HACKING TRUMP

OR, HOW **POTUS**
SUCKER-PUNCHED
AMERICA, TORPEDOED
DEMOCRACY AND
LEFT US A CHOICE:
IMPEACHMENT
OR AUTOCRACY

A WRITER REMEMBERS

RANBIR SIDHU

The Unnamed Press
Los Angeles, CA

The Unnamed Press
P.O. Box 411272
Los Angeles, CA 90041

Published in North America by The Unnamed Press.

1 3 5 7 9 10 8 6 4 2

Copyright © 2018 by Ranbir Sidhu

ISBN: 978-1-944700-78-2

Library of Congress Control Number:

This book is distributed by Publishers Group West

Cover design by Robert Bieselin
Typeset by Jaya Nicely

* * * * * ATTENTION CITIZEN SHOPPERS * * * * *

Your Government is Being Discontinued.

We ~~don't~~ apologize for any inconvenience.

"Our hope is that we can achieve successes and efficiencies for our customers, who are the citizens."[1]

— Jared Kushner, on behalf of
The White House Office of American Innovation

"It's very possible that I could be the first presidential candidate to run and make money on it."[2]

— Donald Trump in 2000

kleptocracy

noun | klep·toc·ra·cy | \klep-'tä-krə-sē\

    plural kleptocracies

1.   :government by those who seek chiefly status and personal gain at the expense of the governed; also :

2.   a particular government of this kind; also :

3.   Rule by thieves, literally.

Table of Contents

* * * * *Disclaimer* * * * *
Message from a Wannabe Dystopia Near You

Full disclosure: I'm writing this from Greece. There are reasons for this.

Over the last few years, I've watched as the country of my parents, India, has spiraled into Hindu nationalist fervor and a rising tolerance for fascism while the one I was born in, the United Kingdom, has cut loose its ties to the rational and set out solo on an around-the-post-truth-world voyage on seas once again frothing with bigotry and violence—the kind I grew up with when I lived there in the 1970s. But watching my adopted home, the United States, where I've lived for much of the past thirty-six years, slide into the huckster embrace of a bigoted reality TV star whose sole lifelong ambition has been to enrich himself and his family is the most heartbreaking—it's like watching a lover die.

I've been following events in the United States mostly from afar—on a Greek island in the Mediterranean, and in the fifth-oldest continuously inhabited city in Europe. The beaches aren't bad either. An economic exile here, and a cultural one from the madness of New York City, where I lived for seventeen years, I've had front-row seats to the downward spiral of another nation in crisis that was hijacked by populists promising the moon and delivering ... well ... a bucketload of steaming crap: a devastated economy, staggering levels of unemployment and poverty, a health care system in ruins where some hospitals can't even afford soap,[3] a judiciary whose independence is continuously being threatened,[4] and a press that's looking more every day like the government's official propaganda mouthpiece.[5] In a recent, well-respected national survey, and after eight long years of nothing but one business after another closing, a staggering 40 percent of surviving Greek businesses believe they'll have to shutter their doors by early 2018 if nothing changes.[6]

The lessons from Greece are clear. When it's naked self-interest and political survival that shape policy, it's not the country that benefits, and certainly not the average Joe or Joan or Yianni or Katerina. In looking back at those first factually dissolute months of the Trump administration, where a new outrage, idiocy, or genuine threat to shared values or democracy seemed to appear almost daily, this book hopes to capture something of the tenor of the times—too much already is vanishing into a collective amnesia brought on by a continuous assault of idiocy, hypocrisy, corruption, and "the crazy"—while also offering a guide, and to some extent a survival manual, for the *small-d* democratic soul.

HACKING TRUMP

OR, HOW **POTUS** SUCKER-PUNCHED AMERICA, TORPEDOED DEMOCRACY AND LEFT US A CHOICE: **IMPEACHMENT** OR AUTOCRACY

Fuck it. We Lost.

Or, an Old Man Burns in a Chair

Days before the November 8 election, while driving through rural New England, I was invited to, of all things, a Guy Fawkes Night celebration—the annual British custom of commemorating the failed plot to blow up the Houses of Parliament by burning an effigy of the lead conspirator—held at a farmhouse in northern Vermont. Champagne bottles were sabered open, a sorta Irish band jammed jigs, and a bearded guy dressed in a kilt wandered around playing the bagpipes. It was a liberal crowd, Hillary and Bernie supporters, with a local Democratic state politician glad-handing among them. The air was charged with a palpable sense of excitement. Everyone *knew* Hillary would ace it, the first woman president. The atmosphere was electric smug celebration. I was one of them, as sure as anyone that The Donald was facing a national kick in the teeth. Believing better of my fellow Americans, I couldn't imagine a majority in this adopted land of mine voting for a bigoted, woman-groping reality TV jackass.

The "Guy" was marched across the yard sitting in a chair and set on the bonfire, where the chair began to burn, and him along with it. He was a crude effigy of Trump—how could he be anyone else? While he burned, and as the crowd whooped and cheered, I found myself filled with rising dread. First the head, then the torso, fell forward.

Watching, I became sure Trump would win. Months of doubts, not only about Clinton's campaign trail failures but about the genuine magnetism of a Trump presidency for much of the electorate, caught up with me and transformed into a bone-deep certainty—no, molecule deep. I mentally argued with myself, then pushed the fear aside. I'd read the polls, gamed out endless electoral college paths to victory, and felt, after thirty-six years spent becoming an American, a visceral understanding of my fellow citizens. This would not happen. When his victory finally happened, I, like many others, felt I'd been flattened by an eighteen-wheeler.

I've thought a lot about that half hour watching the Guy burn. The absolute unquestioning certainty in the faces of my fellow well-meaning liberals, burnished in the firelight, along with their complacent overconfidence, destroyed my conviction in Hillary's coming victory. We couldn't all be so right. Trump did win, even while massively losing the popular vote—and yes, likely pushed over the top by GOP voter suppression tactics and a Rust Belt-targeted Russian fake news campaign.[7] But he shouldn't have come close, and those Rust Belt voters shouldn't have been so disillusioned with national politics to be so easily suckered by the conspiracy-theory sewage spewed out by the right-wing media machine.

My Inner Trumpette

While I believed Hillary Clinton had the potential to be a great president, I felt little love for her phlegmatic, risk-averse plod toward the White House, suspecting we'd see four years of a soft consolidation of

Barack Obama's legacy. Not a bad thing, but certainly not a vision. At least Donald offered razzle-dazzle alongside his racist dog whistles while his promise to shake up the establishment was one promise we were all sure he would keep—that he'd shake it up by digging a few canals in that swamp draining directly into his family's pockets was also obvious. And as much as I *really* did not want to live in Trump's every-kleptocrat's-dream America, I couldn't summon any great enthusiasm for Hillary Clinton's corporate-sponsored wonderland, either.

Driving through rural Maine, New Hampshire, and Vermont, it was impossible not to see the obvious: hundreds, if not thousands, of Trump signs and banners, many handmade, and less than a handful for Clinton, all preprinted, none personalized. These were admittedly Republican counties, and Clinton won all three states, but she won with a genuine lack of enthusiasm. It was a machine politics win in Deep Blue New England. What was also obvious were the shuttered storefronts, the hollowed-out small towns, the rusting cars and trucks in driveways—not a vision of American carnage, but certainly one of a struggling and largely overlooked America, Trump's "forgotten man and woman." One can argue over the hows, the whys, the offered and failed solutions, but it was Trump who spoke to these voters—in the language, for sure, of hidden and not-so-hidden hatred and paranoia-drenched renewal—but he spoke to them nonetheless.

Call it my inner Trumpette, chafing at a narrower and ever-more-shrill discourse on the American left. If the right had punched their ticket to Bonkersville, the left—with its increasing normalization of safe spaces, trigger warnings, the tweet-rage-happy armies of the perennially offended, and as one college administrator recently double-spoke, "empowering a culture of controversy prevention"[8]—looked more and more like they were smoking something mighty strong, and hallucinating America as hipsterville Brooklyn, with an artisanal shoe store on every corner and Grandma and Grandpa in Wyoming talking intersectionality and their cisgendered privilege. No wonder the going-nowhere 4chan nerds flocked to the "alt-right"—the Bubble-Wrap-packed opinions of so many on the left were hardly a welcoming alternative to the shrill cry of victimization rising out of main-stream conservatism.

The Old, Weird America

I was in New York City in the days after November 8. Hardly anyone spoke a word, and if they did, they whispered it, and no one looked you in the eye. We all felt like losers. My own anger bubbled to the point that I wanted to punch every white person I passed on the street—Trump voter or not. I said this out loud to a white friend on a crowded Manhattan subway platform and watched a sea of white faces turn to me with real hostility. I'd grown up in a world drowning in racist violence—Britain in the 1970s, which had its own sour-faced populists and demagogues screaming to make Britain great again by sending the "blackies" and "wogs" and "Pakis" "home." As a kid, racist hooligans tried to knife me, run me over, set me on fire, and, in the worst instance, stuck a blade in my back and pressed me toward an alley, whispering in my ear they were going to skin me alive. I broke free and ran into a crowd. When I eventually left the United Kingdom it was with my brown skin intact. Watching the news of Trump's victory the night of November 8, 2016, I grew afraid my adopted American homeland was heading back to its own violently racist past, and an echo of the world I thought I'd escaped

I got over my brief lapse of sanity without punching anyone, white or otherwise. I realized I was in mourning, like so many others, for an idea of America that had died with the election of Donald Trump. But the America I fell in love with, that impossible-to-define old, weird America, as Greil Marcus called it—hobo America, hitchhiking America, roadhouse America, open road America, flip the bird America, America of the last hope and first dreamer, orphan America, blue collar America of the understated chuckle, America as anthem and melody, whore America and cold-eyed America, ambling heat-haze America of Townes Van Zandt and Willie Dixon, wide-open America of never-ending first acts—was already largely gone when I arrived, if it ever truly existed, having leaked out into regimental subdivisions and homogenous consumer culture. Perhaps what Donald Trump offered, beyond the dog whistles and lines of 100 percent pure Colombian buffoonery, was a hope he might actually overturn the straitjacketed corporatism that had crushed the life out of so much of contemporary experience. This was baloney, of course, but perhaps a tempting fantasy to many who voted for him.

Donald Trump's new, wild America, his Pay-As-U-Go paradise-in-the-making (for the paid, that is) surrenders the common good to our own hardscrabble abilities or lack thereof—or the vagaries of charity—while incentivizing our inner sociopath. Instead of being citizens, we're competing customers, purchasing from our new à la carte government services menu—services outsourced to that slice of corporate America that remains friendly to Trump or as likely Trump Organization subsidiaries. We'll be doing anything and everything to keep our heads above water in "sharing economy" America as ever-larger chunks of our "compassionately untaxed" wages disappear into countless fees and new costs, while a narrow band of the ultra ultra rich retreat to their private clubs, compounds, and penthouses, living out their Versailles fantasies in discreet seclusion.

I.

A Flash of
Military Muscle

*"It is to be regretted that the rich and powerful too often bend
the acts of government to their own selfish purposes."*

Andrew Jackson, Letter to the Senate, 1832

"American Carnage"

January 20, 2017: In a January drizzle in Washington, DC, Donald Trump took the podium to give his inaugural address as president of the United States and offered up, in those first minutes, nothing more than the sickeningly anodyne phrases of patriotic goop. "We will face challenges," he said with all the conviction of a days old slice of toast. "We will confront hardships. But we will get the job done." An AI bot might as well have penned it, programmed to churn out jingoistic mush—and *delivered* it.

Gone was the "bumptious exuberance and slashing humor" that so impressed Camille Paglia[1], replaced by a figure who appeared genuinely insecure about his right to be there. He'd massively lost the popular vote, and spent much of the transition railing against the press and floating conspiracy theories about Democrats and vote rigging— though why rig the vote to deliberately lose, he wouldn't explain.

Fumbles, faux pas, reports of infighting, disorganization, and floundering mismanagement characterized the weeks after November 8, 2016, when in what seemed as much surprise to him as many others, he won crucial Midwest states to propel him to an improbable electoral college victory.

Drops of rain glistened on his suit when, suddenly, a little over a minute into the speech, ten military officers descended the red-and-blue-carpeted stairs and took up positions in two rows immediately behind him. No one could recall a military guard appearing like that during an inaugural, as Maggie Haberman, live-blogging at the *New York Times*, noted.

The moment, almost totally unreported in the press, was upstaged by a cutaway to Barack and Michelle Obama nodding in acknowledgement as Trump thanked them for their efforts in the transition. Another soldier dashed down the stairs, whispered something in the ear of one, and all quickly dispersed, less than a minute after they appeared—a Keystone Cops vision of a protofascist mise-en-scène.

The White House never offered an explanation, but days before, the Pentagon had nixed a Trump request "of including tanks and missile launchers in the inaugural parade." One source said, "They were legit thinking Red Square/North Korea-style parade."[2]

Months earlier, Trump had said something similar. "Military may come marching down Pennsylvania Avenue. That military may be flying over New York City and Washington, DC, for parades. I mean, we're going to be showing our military."[3]

Unable to pull out the seriously big guns, the showman Trump opted for a flash of military muscle and the panache of highly polished insignia to burnish the vapid generalities spilling from his mouth. It was hard to get the image of the soldiers out of your head as he laid out a vision of America as wasteland, a wreck of a nation with "rusted-out factories scattered like tombstones" and "an education system flush with cash, but which leaves our young and beautiful students deprived of knowledge." Behind him, that image kept telling the nation and the world, stood the mightiest military history has ever known.

"Where Reagan smoothed the rougher edges of his vision with soaring patriotic imagery," wrote NBC's Benjy Sarlin, "Trump walked down a dark dystopia in which crime, joblessness and foreign exploitation had laid the country low while a shadowy elite profited at every turn. ... [He] did little to reassure Americans opposed to his candidacy. And far from lowering the sky-high expectations he set on the trail, he raised them in bold terms that could haunt him if he fails to meet his own standards. At one point, he promised to 'eradicate completely from the face of the earth' the threat of 'radical Islamic terrorism.'"[4]

"Robbed our country," "unrealized potential," "crime and drugs," "mothers and children trapped in poverty," "one nation," "their pain is our pain," "one heart, one hope, one glorious destiny."

Through it all, his party-piece line, "The American carnage stops right here and stops right now,"[5] shone all the light anyone needed into the heart of the speech's intent—erecting the straw man of a truly devastated America that needed the unbreakable will of a great hero to rebuild and renew it— making it feel more like a Freudian slipstream of a speech.

The dual wordsmiths of this American chauvinistic diarrhea, Trump campaign honchos and "alt-right" masterminds Steve Bannon and Steve Miller[6] turned the achievements of the first African American president violently on their head, seeing sickness and decay where there was growth and possibility and blind to all that had happened in the eight years since America's, and the world's, most destructive economic crisis after the Great Depression.

There are times you can almost hear thirty-one-year-old Stephen Miller aching, after all these years, to punch some teenage La Raza activist at his old Santa Monica high school in the jaw—or Steve Bannon, Harley-riding bad-boy-turned-Islamophobe, throbbing to push Trump to press the button and *bomb bomb bomb* the Muslims.

"The time for empty talk is over. Now arrives the hour of action."

Hidden in plain sight among the hollow dictums that could have been lifted from second-rate *Lord of the Rings* fan fiction is a picture of America that is so at odds with reality it's hard not to look at it as projection—the America Donald Trump *needs* to see and *wants* to see, his own empty-souled reality star self-graffitied in apocalyptic monotones across a complex and vibrant nation. Lacking a genuine crisis, he was forced to invent one. To hammer through his violently extremist agenda, he needed to raise the stakes considerably further. Even George W. Bush left the dais baffled, according to three witnesses who overheard his reaction: "That was some weird shit."[7]

"From this moment on, it's going to be America first... America will start winning again, winning like never before."

Difficult to imagine how the America First motto, the 1930s feel-good slogan of American Nazi sympathizers, which the Anti-Defamation League warned Trump last year to stop using because of its bigoted and violent history,[8] was NOT aimed at open racists among Trump supporters. As the divergence between rhetoric and reality—the promises made and actionable plans—widens, the die-hards will only be strengthened in their refusal to look squarely at the non-post-truth world the rest of us are still trying very hard to live in.

"We will bring back our jobs. We will bring back our borders. We will bring back our wealth. And we will bring back our dreams."

Donald Trump's plan—a prescription of staggeringly lower taxes, massive military expansion, and the destruction of what little safety nets the United States has left for the poor and elderly—could be spelled out in the all-caps scribble of the eat-the-poor far-right's resident madwoman in the attic, Ayn Rand. In her dystopian novel *Anthem*, Rand described the horror show of a statist, collectivist world where the word "I" doesn't exist, where people are referred to as numbers, and it's a crime to think independently and especially outside the "vocation" assigned to you by the state. Based on her experiences growing up under the nightmare of Soviet Union's early years, this is the vision that many on the far right claim, as much out of self-interest as ideology, that the American left is leading the country toward—and one that Rand's followers are valiantly fighting against.

Their cure—unsurprisingly cathartic to the ultra-wealthy donors funding the political campaigns, think tanks, and foundations peddling the endless tax-cut snake oil—is to starve the government of oxygen, which in this case is money, until all it can perform are the truly bare essentials.

Goodbye Citizenship.

Hello the New American Customer-Driven Government.

An America for the truly wealthy while the rest of us, no longer citizens but mere customers of the new "sharing economy" Pay-As-U-Go government, struggle under the floorboards of their mansions in a dog-eat-dog underworld, which is also the agenda of the hard-right

Republican Congress, spearheaded by the Speaker of the House, internet "hottie" and choir boy Paul Ryan—the GOP's Ken Doll publicist spouting the *black is white* lies rationalizing its eat-the-poor agenda. Add to that Trump's former campaign manager, alt-right guru and since ousted chief strategist Stephen Bannon, and between the three of them you have the formidable unibrow on the Neanderthal face of the modern GOP body politic. While Bannon has moved offices back to the far-right Breitbart News Network, where he acts as bad-cop nationalist goad, Ryan remains the good cop in the backbiting snake pit that's become the Trump administration. The ideas of both men remain central not only to Trump's thinking, but to those of whom he surrounds himself—the billionaire self-declared elect who've decided this is their country, not ours, and they've finally found the one man who can take it back for them and make it the playground for the ultra ultra rich they've always wanted.

II.
The WrestleMania Presidency

"It will be equally forgotten that the vigor of government is essential to the security of liberty; that, in the contemplation of a sound and well-informed judgment, their interest can never be separated; and that a dangerous ambition more often lurks behind the specious mask of zeal for the rights of the people than under the forbidden appearance of zeal for the firmness and efficiency of government. History will teach us that the former has been found a much more certain road to the introduction of despotism than the latter, and that of those men who have overturned the liberties of republics, the greatest number have begun their career by paying an obsequious court to the people; commencing demagogues, and ending tyrants."

Alexander Hamilton, The Federalist Papers, 1787

The spectacle is the message...

To misquote Marshall McLuhan, who summed up our age with the phrase, "The medium is the message." Spectacle is Trump's medium. It's the language he speaks, and if a Trump presidency tells us anything, it is that language has lost meaning and all we are left with is the unchecked theater of power.

"WHAT'S GOING ON OVER HERE?!!"

Donald J. Trump, moments before
body-slamming Vince McMahon, 04/01/07

There's perhaps no better arena to understand the spectacle at the heart of Donald Trump than the modern faux wrestling ring, where the fights are staged, the punches pulled (unless it's the Don), and when blood spills it's either fake or planned.

"He loved the sensationalism, the drama, the fantasy."

Sam Nunberg, former Trump campaign aide[1]

Trump first became involved in professional wrestling in the 1980s, when he was looking to gain press for his expanding casino empire in Atlantic City and Las Vegas. It was a match made in heaven, as the savvy Trump would learn, palling around with billionaire Vince Mc-Mahon, owner of what was then the WWF but later became the WWE. Both enterprises benefited, though the WWE far more than Trump's bankrupt Atlantic City casinos—the *New York Times*'s Russ Buettner and Charles V. Bagli call them "a protracted failure" where "Trump put up little of his own money, shifted personal debts to the casinos and collected millions of dollars in salary, bonuses and other payments. The burden of his failures fell on investors and others who had bet on his business acumen."[2]

In moving from the sidelines to center stage, and becoming an "actor" instead of a spectator, The Donald began to understand something of the power that comes from physically entering the ring. What he learned was invaluable, for here he took the no-holds-barred bravado of his business persona and honed it on the stage of blue collar angst and desire, the billionaire slumming with the plebes, and discovering what it's like to experience the adulation of crowds. If he didn't solve their problems, at least he gave them an evening's entertaining salve to lessen the blows of mortgage payments, health care bills, car insurance, low-wage jobs and their kids' demolished expectations. Here was a church, if ever there was one, but with megaton speakers and lights that'd burn your eyes out—and yes, genuine, family fare escapism.

"Babyface"

"Trump connoted wealth and a no-guff, take-no-prisoners attitude, said Michael Axelrod, a Long Island fan," writes Josh Dawsey, "who added that he remembered few other billionaire-types jousting in the ring. 'People who go to wrestling matches don't tend to like people who make more in one day than they make in their lifetimes,' Axelrod said. **'But he didn't take sh-- from anyone and made his own rules, and people seem to like that in their wrestling characters.'** In wrestling terms, he was known as a 'babyface,' or good guy, Axelrod said, adding he'd never seen him booed at a wrestling event. **'I don't think he would have liked getting booed,'** Axelrod said."[3]

At the heart of *WrestleMania* is one simple proposition: *we* the good are threatened by *they* the bad, and if a hero does not step forward to save us, all will be lost. In the convoluted good-vs-evil soap opera story lines, outsized characters and costumes and raucous crowds booing the *bad hombres* and cheering the *white knight heroes*, Donald Trump found a language he could use, the modern in-your-face, kick-your-butt, the-walls-are-crashing-all-around-us spectacle.

"I would say to him," Sam Nunberg said, "we're going to be the WWE of the [presidential] primary with the smash-mouth adrenaline pumping."[4]

Trump used lessons learned in years of appearances at WWE events to nuclear effect in the 2016 campaign, inventing enemies and scapegoats while painting himself as the *only hero* able to save the nation. It was a convincing, well-acted shtick, and one he mastered in the fantasy arenas of steroid-drenched men in colorful tights and overblown costumes who were able to punch each other without a single blow actually landing.

"Professional wrestling is fake. Trump's punches weren't."

... as Travis Waldron summed up in the *Huffington Post*. When Donald Trump, in the middle of the fabled Battle of the Billionaires, clothes-lined his opponent Vince McMahon to the floor and started pummeling, every fist connected with all the force our Bully-in-Chief could muster.

It was Waldron who wrote the definitive history of that bout—and bout it was. Months of setup, of creating story lines and characters, of a weekly amping of the crowd to a greater frenzy. On the night itself, Trump had money rain down from the ceiling to delirious fans—not his money, of course, these were all McMahon's Jeffersons and Franklins, but no one was told this.

Trump, in Waldron's words, played the role of "the magnanimous billionaire, the one who understood what they wanted." *They* being the mostly blue-collar audience, genuine Red State NASCAR America, an audience Trump was only beginning to learn how to play to and manipulate using nothing more than the senses-shearing glamour of over-the-top spectacle. He was on *their* side, a bonafide billionaire who knew how the system worked from the inside and therefore knew how to stick it to the elites, embodied during that bout by the evil billionaire owner of WWE, Vince MaMahon. It was a role Trump was learning to enjoy

When Trump finally toppled McMahon, he never pulled a punch, never once gave it to him easy. If anything was real that night, this was it, and maybe that's all we need to know about the man: when he promises to pull his punches, he never does.[5] And when he gives us what he thinks is stage-managed spectacle, it's an open question whether he knows the difference, or whether it even matters to him that there's a line between reality and fantasy.

... and the spectacle is hollow

In 2002, filmmaker Errol Morris interviewed Donald Trump about his favorite movie, Orson Welles's 1941 masterpiece *Citizen Kane*, in part of a series with renowned businessmen and heads of state, including Donald Rumsfeld and Mikhail Gorbachev.

The movie, a portrait of media magnate William Randolph Hearst, chronicles the toxic, violent combustion that ignites when unspeakable wealth meets a talented but ultimately empty soul. "It was an attack on property," Welles said in a 1960 interview. "And on acquisition of property... **And on the corruption of an acquisitive society where a man of real gifts, and real charm, and real humanity destroys himself and everything near him.**"[6]

Trump recognized nothing of the monstrosity, of the failure of humanity, of the genuine darkness into which Kane's soul descended at the movie's end. Instead he found his shadow self, glittering in moody black and white high on the silver screen, and the faint glow of an object lesson.

"I think you learn in [*Citizen*] *Kane* that maybe wealth isn't everything," he told Morris, "because he had the wealth, but he didn't have the happiness. The table getting larger and larger and larger with he and his wife getting further and further apart as he got wealthier and wealthier. Perhaps I can understand that."[7]

For the first few months of the Trump administration, that table stretched from 1600 Pennsylvania Avenue, Washington, DC, where Donald Trump lives, all the way to the corner of Fifth Avenue and 56th Street, Manhattan, where his wife, Melania, was living. How long it stretches now, in the echoing halls of the president's private quarters, who knows?

"There was a great rise in Citizen Kane, and there was a modest fall. The fall wasn't a financial fall, the fall was a personal fall, but it was a fall

nevertheless. So you have the highs, and you had the lows."

Donald Trump on *Citizen Kane*, 2002[8]

Knock knock, is anyone even freakin' home?!

Not really, says Errol Morris.

"I'm Jewish, and I used to describe Rumsfeld to people as the least Jewish person I'd ever met: no guilt, no self-loathing, no remorse, no self-doubt, no nothing," Morris later said, talking of the interview. "Just a kind of glib self-satisfaction—which I see with Trump, by the way. **A glib kind of narcissistic self-love, almost like he's masturbating in public.** And it's kind of gross. I don't know how else to describe it."[9]

How to sum up a man who sees in a monster only a halfway flattering reflection of himself? Morris went to Argentine writer Jorge Luis Borges, who once wrote the line that perhaps best captures our new Orangehead-in-Chief:

"There's nothing more frightening than a labyrinth without a center."

How about a president without so much as a fundamental grip on reality? At his first solo presser, held (or more accurately performed) three weeks after the inauguration, Donald Trump took the podium and showed us, once again, that the man we elected pulls "facts" out of thin air and could care less that we knew this, all of it served up in one hour and seventeen minutes of straight-up 180-proof, unadulterated Trumptini—shaken *and* stirred.

In a performance that many news organizations described as "unhinged," he told us that "Russia is fake news"; that "this thing called nuclear weapons like lots of things are done with uranium including some bad things;" that he'd been "briefed" and because of that knew that a "nuclear holocaust would be like no other;" openly implied that all black people knew all other black people; attacked an Orthodox Jewish reporter for asking about reports of rising anti-Semitism; adopted an oddly robotic pose to proclaim, loudly, that "we are going to attack Mosul in four months" as the reason he never says this; snidely mocked the reporter from the BBC, saying "Here's another beauty;" claimed CNN was no longer "fake news" but "very fake news" and bitched about what he called "so much anger and hatred and just the hatred" on the network; wound himself up into extraordinary word pretzels trying to get out of answering questions about the just-fired Mike Flynn and his own ties to Russia and Vladimir Putin; mocked Hillary Clinton's attempted reset with Russia eight (!) years ago; and among countless other falsehoods, prevarications, jabs and insults, openly lied about the size of his electoral college victory and when called on it excused himself by passively retorting, "I was given that information."

Even Fox News's Shep Smith, poster boy for All Things Ill-Considered, went on a tear eviscerating the president.

"He keeps repeating ridiculous throwaway lines that are not true at all and sort of avoiding this issue of Russia as if we're some kind of fools for asking the question. Really? We're fools for asking the questions? No sir, we are not fools for asking the questions. And we demand to know the answer to this question."[10]

But in one comment, that went largely unreported, buried under the fast collapsing bluster and widening anarchy, he talked again about his favorite topic, or:

How I Won the Election:

"I won with news conferences and probably speeches. I certainly didn't win by people listening to you people. ... I'm having a good time. Tomorrow, they will say, 'Donald Trump rants and raves at the press.' I'm not ranting and raving. I'm just telling you. You know, you're dishonest people. ... I love this. I'm having a good time doing it."

He was right. The subject had changed, the press would now move on. Russia, potential illegality, any talk of treason, etc.—it all died, at least temporarily, with that performance.

"Trump's detractors immediately panned the show as madness," Michael Goodwin put it in the *New York Post*, "but **they missed the method behind it and proved they still don't understand his appeal.** Facing his first crisis in the Oval Office, he was unbowed in demonstrating his bare-knuckle intention to fight back."[11] "It was a dizzying performance," David Catanese summed up, "that demonstrated **[Trump's] singular ability to reshuffle the direction of the coverage with a spectacle**... It will infuriate his critics and energize his supporters... Vintage Trump."[12]

Gone were the #Kremlingate stories, the calls for investigations, the damaging press on his imploding cabinet. At this critical juncture, in the early weeks of his presidency, more of this would have genuinely eroded support among his base. If there was a time to knee-cap him politically, it was these few weeks while he was still struggling to understand the magnitude of the job he had just signed up for—and if we were ever going to have a press pounding out 24/7 the drumbeat of collusion with the Russians—as they did with Bill Clinton during the Monica Lewinsky scandal—this was the moment. Instead we got the retina-sheering glare of spotlights on the madman, no-holds-barred, bare-knuckle brawler in the pit, hiding all else and blinding us, once again, to the real story.

The Cat Video Industrial Complex?

Let's leave it to *The Atlantic*'s Megan Garber who, while she didn't use the term, is my go-to expert on the rise of the **Cat Video Industrial Complex**.

"The primacy of the screen in our current method of candidate-screening has meant that politics is, at this point, largely indistinguishable from pop culture. Celebrified candidates are part of the compact Americans have made with their political news, because policy can be boring and learning the new things requires understanding the old ones and the stakes are so high and voters are all very human and tired. **Attention is one of the most powerful things Americans have to give**; news outlets reward them for it not just with pertinent information about 'the issues,' but also with juicy soundbites and indignation-inducing video clips and distractingly delightful comparisons of candidates to cats."[13]

Or while we swoon ever more giddily before the dopamine-spiking distractions of cats face-planting to take our minds off increasingly time-stressed lives and daily let our attention spans get sliced and diced into narrower bands by the predatory algorithms of Silicon Valley startups—which have moved on from making us the product and now monetize momentary bursts of our deep-stem neurological engagement—we no longer have time for emotion, only reactive sentiment, leaving us twisting in the wind of our own deep-set prejudices—and easy pickings for the first demagogue to walk along.

Mee-ooow!

III.
The Rise of Honey Badger

"[Political parties] may now and then answer popular ends, they are likely in the course of time and things, to become potent engines, by which cunning, ambitious, and unprincipled men will be enabled to subvert the power of the people and to usurp for themselves the reins of government, destroying afterwards the very engines which have lifted them to unjust dominion."

George Washington, Farewell Address, 1796

BIRTH CONTROL MAKES WOMEN UNATTRACTIVE AND CRAZY

Breitbart.com, December 8, 2015

One of many such headlines—this one provided by multiple boy-band-reject and fascist-fashion victim Milo Yiannopoulos—that appeared on Breitbart.com's homepage during Steve Bannon's tenure as head honcho.

A cesspool of misogyny, conspiracy, and homophobia, *Breitbart*'s headlines alone feed a near-continuous thirst among the right's most credulous bottom-feeders and outrage junkies. "The Solution to On-line 'Harassment' is Simple: Women Should Log Off," "Lesbian Bridezillas Bully Bridal Shop Owner Over Religious Beliefs," "Roger Stone: Huma Abedin 'Most Likely a Saudi Spy' with 'Deep, Inarguable Connections' to 'Global Terrorist Entity,'" "Gay Rights Have Made Us Dumber, it's Time to Get Back in the Closet,"—and let's not forget the openly anti-Semitic "Bill Kristol: Republican Spoiler, Renegade Jew."

From such illustrious journalistic beginnings, Bannon was catapulted onto the national stage as the new campaign manager (number three if you were counting) in August 2016 for the then wildly floundering Donald Trump's presidential bid, along with future Chief Propagandist Kellyanne Conway and (briefly) Roger Ailes—this last a natural fit in Pussy Grabber's posse as he'd just been dumped by Fox News after multiple allegations of sexual harassment.

Bannon—a former sucker on an arm of the Goldman Sachs Vampire Squid and Hollywood dropout with multiple millions in the bank was brought in to right the fast-sinking ship of the *SS Trumptanic*, which had hit, that summer, the iceberg of genuine GOP hatred of the man and his flailing campaign.[1]

Bannon's plan was simple: *Release the Trumpken!*

Kick the handlers to the curb, shred the prepared remarks, throw out the tele-prompters—LET TRUMP BE TRUMP.

Yeah, we were all there, mocked, laughed, wasted hours making silly GIFs and shared Obama and Joe Biden memes, posted links to Facebook about the coming #Trumplosion or #Trumpmageddon, how we'd dance on his campaign's ashes while, invisibly, Steve Bannon was working behind the scenes to inject the right level of hate-filled populism, outright falsehoods, and enough bullshit about Hillary Clinton to expand Trump's base beyond the loathsome bubble of David Duke lifers.

Few thought it would work. Not Trump. Not Bannon. Probably not even a preternaturally overconfident Kellyanne Conway, who crowed maniacally with a Cheshire Cat fuck you each time her candidate's numbers tanked.

But it did work. And here we are.

So who is Stephen K. Bannon? Well, briefly he was …

"The Second Most Powerful Man in World..."

... so *Time* magazine dubbed him...[2]

... or #PresidentBannon as he was known in the Twitterverse. And while that might have changed, his worldview still holds sway in the freshly paranoia-repainted walls of the West Wing ...

Since taking the helm of *Breitbart News*, after its founding editor Andrew Breitbart died unexpectedly in 2012, he transformed the already oversized noxious far-right blog, which even then was little more than a clickbait dump drawing meth-addled traffic from *Drudge Report* junkies, into a venue for bullying, sensationalism, fake news, racism, a never-ending stream of whack-job conspiracy theories, and a Klaxon screeching the imminent doom of virile white manhood—and, with the rise of Trump, a channel for pure Trump propaganda.

Ben Shapiro, a former Breitbart writer, described the new Breitbart as **"Trump's personal *Pravda"***—referring to the old official mouthpiece of the Communist Party in the former Soviet Union—and went on, describing Bannon as nothing more than a **"scorched-earth opportunist."**[3]

By hiring Bannon, says Sarah Posner, Trump was "**signaling a whole-hearted embrace of the 'alt-right,' a once-motley assemblage of anti-immigrant, anti-Muslim, ethno-nationalistic provocateurs** who have coalesced behind Trump and curried the GOP nominee's favor on social media. In short, Trump has embraced the core readership of *Breitbart News*."[4]

As Bannon himself proudly admitted when interviewed at the Republican National Convention in July 2016[5]:

"We're the platform for the alt-right."

According to David Von Drehle, Bannon and Trump "share the experience of being talkative and brash, **pugnacious money magnets who never quite fit among the elite.** A Democrat by heritage and Republican by choice, Bannon has come to see both parties as deeply corrupt, a belief that has shaped his recent career as a polemical filmmaker and Internet bomb thrower."[6]

But it's all cool, because …

"Honey Badger don't give a shit"

Breitbart's heart—and Bannon's—is reflected in a viral video that hit social media newsfeeds around the time of Bannon's takeover. "Over a piece of old nature footage a clever narrator commented on a single-minded beast known as a honey badger. Through bee stings, snakebites, and other degradations, the animal never stops killing and eating. 'Honey Badger don't give a shit,' the narrator summed up." Bannon stole the phrase to use as his personal motto.[7]

"Lenin wanted to destroy the state, and that's my goal too. I want to bring everything crashing down, and destroy all of today's establishment."

Stephen Bannon, November 12, 2013[8]

Like a sallow-faced emo goth still living in Mommie's basement, Bannon's combustible imaginative life never seems to stray far from the apocalyptic. That he's well-read is undisputed, and he can cite a litany of thinkers from the heretic Giordano Bruno to the Italian fascist Julius Evola, but like many emotionally stunted self-styled intellectuals, he's unequal to the task of actually stitching together not only the consequences of his ideas, but blind to any facts that fail to reflect his self-interest.

In his 2010 movie, *Generation Zero,* which centers on 2008 banking crisis he offers up, according to Micah Sifry, "90 minutes of often lurid images from the last hundred years of world history, interspersed with interviews with a seemingly never-ending array of conservative intellectuals, nearly all of them white men, **Bannon's script offers a coherent and hellishly bleak vision of our past, present, and future, driven by a magical belief in historical determinism.**" The ultimate blame for the crisis is not on the bankers or lax regulation or an out of control GOP, but the *liberals and hippies* who've hijacked American exceptionalism since the end of World War Two.[9]

And it's this order Bannon wants to destroy: the entire postwar American liberal tradition.

Pinning the blame on the New Deal and the extravaganza of liberal big government overspending and regulation it gave birth to in the decades following, Bannon argues that only after the walls of the modern welfare state come crashing down will the hard-nosed American entrepreneur be truly freed to build not only a new world, but genuine personal wealth—or, as economist Amity Shlaes describes him in the movie, "the man who pays, the man who prays, the man who is not thought of, the forgotten man." It's a vision that John Saward describes as little more than "ethno-nationalist bathroom stall graffiti shined up to look like crystal-ball prognostication."[10]

"The world is on fire... all of a sudden it's going to dawn on people, this is not a problem for guys in the Middle East: This is a problem for you in Kansas City."

Stephen Bannon, *Vice News*[11]

Much like Donald Trump's YA dystopian inaugural address—which Bannon largely penned—where the newly minted president saw nothing but "American carnage" across the cities and streets of the nation, Bannon finds little else but whiny Jews, murderous Muslims, stealing blacks, and everywhere, immigrants, legal and illegal, taking the rightful jobs of upstanding white Americans.

Talking to Reid Cherlin in 2014, Bannon took him on a full-on roller-coaster tour of his conspiracy-blighted mind.

Ten whole counties were under full Mexican drug cartel control, he told Cherlin, a fact that only the diligence of Breitbart Texas exposed. "It'll blow your fucking mind," Bannon said. **"We'll take you on shit in Laredo and these other places; you literally will think, "I can't be in America."** US immigration policy was built, Bannon argued, to undermine the labor market. "When you flood the zone, as Jeff Sessions says, with 50 million workers…" He ranted on, about Ebola's spread in West Africa being due to the negligence of President Obama, absurdly claiming, "By the way, he's never been briefed [on the virus]."[12]

The Fourth Turning… or whatever— *Google it*

Like all good conspiracy nuts, Bannon needed a theory upon which to hang his ever-expanding whack-jobbery. He found it in pop historians William Strauss and Neil Howe who theorize that history moves in 80- 100-year cycles, or "saecula," which come to fiery ends in an "ekpyrosis"—conspiracy nuts do love their randomly interchangeable Latin and Greek—or, basically fire and brimstone raining from the heavens until the old is killed and a new order rises from the ashes (this latter being Bannon's cheery interpretation!)[13]

And you know where we are? **You guessed it! We are right on the edge of the fire and brimstone.**

In a talk at a Vatican conference in the summer of 2014 given via internet link, Bannon expanded on his views.

"We're at the very beginning stages of a very brutal and bloody conflict ... if the people in this room, the people in the church, do not bind together ... to fight for our beliefs against this new barbarity that's starting, that will completely eradicate everything that we've been bequeathed over the last 2,000, 2,500 years."

For Bannon, the major wars of the twentieth century have been about a "Judeo-Christian West versus atheists" while the "underlying principle is an enlightened form of capitalism, that capitalism really gave us the wherewithal."

He added, "I believe we've come partly offtrack in the years since the fall of the Soviet Union and we're starting now in the 21st century, which I believe, strongly, is a crisis both of our church, a crisis of our faith, a crisis of the West, a crisis of capitalism."[14]

In summing up, he firmly placed where he believed the heart of the coming conflict would be:

"We are in an outright war against jihadist Islamic fascism. And this war is, I think, metastasizing far quicker than governments can handle it."

It's a theme Bannon continually returns to: **"Our big belief, one of our central organizing principles at the site, is that we're at war."**[15]

But why hitch your wagon to Trump, a godless, if charismatic, jackass with the attention span of dehydrated amoeba? Well, Bannon's never been shy of explaining that one, as he told *Vanity Fair* in 2016, calling...[16]

Trump a "blunt instrument for us... I don't know whether he really gets it or not."

With Steve Bannon's August 2017 ouster from the hallowed halls of the West Wing and return to his kingmaker role as crazy-in-chief over at Breitbart, he's become again the outsider bad cop nationalist goad, more bluntly echoing and pushing the extremist edges of the most virulent aspects of Donald Trump's agenda, and pushing Trump and his cohorts to follow through on those. Or, put another way: don't believe the hype that he was fired, because in effect he never left, he just moved desks and became the at-large mad hatter propagandist for all things Trumpian, shoveling the same shit, just using a different shovel.

IV.
The Apotheosis
of Ayn Rand

"Talents for low intrigue, and the little arts of popularity, may alone suffice to elevate a man to the first honors in a single State."

Alexander Hamilton, The Federalist Papers, 1788

Atlas (Sorta) Shrugged Chapter One— *The Theme*

"Who is Paul Ryan?"

The light was ebbing, and Eddie Willers could not distinguish the bum's face. The bum had said it simply, without expression. But from the sunset far at the end of the street, yellow glints caught his eyes, and the eyes looked straight at Eddie Willers, mocking and still—as if the question had been addressed to…

the causeless uneasiness within him…

Or whatever. You get the picture…

Of course, the bum in the opening line of *Atlas Shrugged* doesn't ask who Paul Ryan is—he asks who John Galt is, the so-called hero of that unwieldy slab of buttered-up prose, half-baked, juvenile philosophizing, and Nietzschean ubermanliness that is the writing of Ayn

Rand. The Borg Queen of modern libertarian conservatism and the ill-fitting atheist at the zombie heart of the hard-nosed capitalist wing of the Christian right, she is a surprising standard-bearer for the God-above-country nationalists who populate the Oh-So-White Pages of Modern "Medicare is Communism I mean Satanism!" Right-wingery these days.

But wait, God above country for sure, but Mammon above God...

Mercilessly dividing the world into the "makers" and the "takers"—or the wealth creators and the rest of us leaches—Rand's philosophy argued for a form of enlightened selfishness and free-for-all capitalism where looking out for others was the one sure way to sabotage your own bliss.[1]

Rand found a fanboy in the youthful Paul Ryan's *causeless uneasiness*—**"I grew up reading Ayn Rand,"** Ryan told a gathering of Ayn Rand superfans in 2005, **"and it taught me quite a bit about who I am and what my value systems are, and what my beliefs are."**[2]

A Separate Unreality

One of the genuine contradictions of the modern right is how far it has been able to pervert the Christian message of charity, humility and service to its own unashamedly capitalist ends. In this newborn Christianity, charity is theft, humility becomes bombast, and service is lost to naked self-interest.

The Calvinist heart of this message—that the elect of God shall inherit the earth and its wealth and the rest shall suffer the mark of poverty and eternal damnation—was the crack that allowed an openly atheist philosopher to become Christian capitalism's go-to theorist: for in the rewards of Randian selfishness lie the evidence of God's grace, and the "failures" of poverty its opposite. Translate this into Paul Ryan's brand of contemporary GOP politics and you get a made-to-order rationalization of the worst excesses that capitalism, in its most brutal forms, can wreak on a populace and a fundamentally Christian argument to shred the safety net. Without it, the elect, through their God-given grace and talents, will rise to the top while the rest of us will be marked openly as the damned—and why feed and house the damned when that money can go to the godly elect?

The shotgun marriage of American Christianity and kick-the-poor capitalism, one that Steve Bannon happily accompanied down the aisle, gave the hard right of the modern GOP an easy-to-digest transcendent mythology that, instead of softening their vision, gave it an unforgiving blade edge. Who needs safety nets when you have the arms of Baby Jesus to raise you up? And who needs Social Security when, if you were a genuine Christian, you'd have spent your productive years not helping others but filling endless bucketloads with cash and wisely reinvesting? A true Christian would have spared others the need to help him. Regulations, bureaucracy, and money wasted on the poor and sick all stood in the way of the ambitions of a wise, self-interested Christian businessman and investor, and his relationship not only with money, but with God.[3]

So his Christianity rubs off as easily as the gilt on the custom-ordered family bible.

The Three Big Lies of Paul Ryan

1. He's the real thing, a GOP billion-dollar-brain.

Let's not forget the all-inquiring intellect, as Fred Barnes at *The Weekly*

Standard tells us: "His motto is, 'Inquire, inquire, inquire, read, read, read.' **He has made himself an expert on the budget, taxes, and health care.** Ryan knows more about the federal budget than anyone else on Capitol Hill and talks about it more fluently."[4]

The noted conservative historian Paul Rahe not only orgasmed, but widely spattered the ceiling, in his verbal bacchanal praising Ryan. "He has attained a stature that no Congressman in my lifetime has achieved," he writes. "When I cast my mind back in the past in search of comparable figures, I can come up with only two—James Madison in the First Federal Congress, and Henry Clay, when he was Speaker of the House. There were no doubt others, but the list is not long, and I doubt whether there would be anyone on it who served in the last hundred years."[5]

Brain-Drained

Facts tell a different story.

His showcase "Ryan Budgets"—which resurrected the imaginary bogeyman of an imminent debt crisis to massively cut spending—were charitably called "magical"[6] and a "War Against Math."[7] It was little more than an unabashed massive tax cut for the wealthy—really the uberwealthy—on the backs of, you guessed it, working families, the poor, senior citizens, schools, the arts, the environment … etc. The 2013 budget, if enacted, would have blown a "$6.7 trillion hole" in the national debt while claiming to save "$4.6 trillion over the next ten years … Ryan's magical savings are 146 percent of his overall savings."[8]

Yeah, Ryan's a bright fellow—he knows how to expertly spin a devastating lie that benefits his billionaire buddies while screwing the nation's elderly and poor.

2. He's an anti-poverty crusader.

During the 2012 campaign, Paul Ryan pushed Mitt Romney to talk more about poverty in America, taking to the road himself on a nationwide tour, as described in the *National Review*'s hagiographic portrait, where Ryan comes off as cousin-once-removed from Mother Teresa (or that long-haired hippie she prayed to). "On October 24, 2012, Ryan met with 20 grassroots leaders at Cleveland State University," Ian Tuttle writes, "to learn about anti-poverty strategies that were working in their communities... At the end of a series of testimonials—people telling stories of redemption after bouts of drug abuse or stints in prison—the activists asked Ryan if they could lay hands on him. 'I could see the tears in Paul's eyes,' says [organizer Bob] Woodson, 'and also in the eyes of the Secret Service agents.'"[9]

Poverty Schmoverty

He talks a good line, lets himself bathe in a ray of heavenly light once in a while, but as Jonathan Weisman wrote in his profile, the actual impact of his policies on those people he claims to want to help would be devastating. "I'm stunned by how oblivious he is to the pain his policies would cause people," said David R. Obey, a Wisconsin Democrat who often battled his downstate colleague. "What amazes me is that someone that nice personally has such a cold, almost academic view of what the impact of his policies would be on people."[10] While the *New Republic*'s Danny Vinik called Ryan's proposed 2014 budget cuts "cruel" to the nation's most needy, while using "the premise of a debt crisis as an excuse to cut services and support for low-income Americans."[11]

3. He is that genuine unicorn in today's Washington, a bipartisan Republican.

Here is Ryan talking about himself in his 2012 heyday: "What I hope happens is we go to the country with a positive agenda to show how we will prevent a debt crisis, how we will get this economy growing again," he said, **"then win the House, Senate and the White House, and then be magnanimous in that victory and include reformers from the other side of the aisle into a coalition to fix these problems."**[12]

Sore Ass Winner...

... or plain old liar?

What a difference actually winning makes. Four years later and now that the GOP has won the House, Senate, and White House, Ryan sings a very different tune.

"House Speaker Paul Ryan is bluntly promising to ram a partisan agenda through Capitol Hill..." Ben Weyl warned in late 2016, "with Obamacare repeal and trillion-dollar tax cuts likely at the top of the list. And Democrats would be utterly defenseless to stop them. **Typically, party leaders offer at least the pretense of seeking bipartisanship when discussing their policy plans. But Ryan is saying frankly that Republicans would use budget reconciliation—a powerful procedural tool—to bypass Democrats entirely.**"[13]

And given the chance, Ryan always returns to partisan hackdom: "His biggest opportunity for compromise came in late 2010 when, as a member of the president's bipartisan deficit-reduction commission, he had a chance to vote on the $4 trillion plan put forward by the commission's chairmen, Erskine B. Bowles and Alan K. Simpson. He voted no, taking every House Republican on the panel with him and preventing the guarantee of a vote in Congress."[14]

So how did this flapdoodle ideologue bird effigy on the battle flag of the drooling, straitjacket battalion of the GOP become the "sane" face of the Republican Party?

Brownnoser Makes Good

In the end, one thing and one thing only is guaranteed to get you far in a truly fat-ass town like DC ...

... and that's some serious ass-kissing.

"There's a reason that Ryan's high-school classmates voted him the 'biggest brownnoser' in 1988," explains Theo Anderson. "**Living by principles means making hard choices. Ryan has built his career by consistently avoiding them.** It's more precise to say that Ryan has commitments that pull him in opposing directions and, when forced to choose between them, he always chooses the path that will increase his power. **Kissing up to the GOP's kingmakers and brownnosing the party's base are the principles he lives by.**"[15]

There seems to be no love lost between Paul Ryan and Donald Trump—both have sparred openly, Trump calling the speaker "weak and ineffective"[16] and Ryan refusing to attend campaign events with the future groper-in-chief.[17] Their current truce, like a medieval marriage of convenience between warring clans, has each viewing the other as little more than a convenient tool.

Their common goal? Well that's simple:

Drown the Baby

The "baby" in this case being the government.

... or Grover Norquist's Fever Dream

Aside from Ronald Reagan, perhaps no single individual was more responsible for the unholy marriage of fuck-you capitalism and the extremist wings of Christian fundamentalism than Grover Norquist, founder and head since 1985 of policy tank and lobbying shop Americans for Tax Reform. Hardly a Bible-thumper himself (he's married to a Muslim and is openly supportive of gay and minority rights), he realized early that to achieve his goal, as he told NPR in 2001…[18]

…to shrink government "to the size where I can drag it into the bathroom and drown it in the bathtub…"

... he would need more than the perpetual Capitol Hill tax-cut hecklers in his corner.

Faith, Guns & Taxes

The coalition he built, with **"the guy who wants to be left alone to practice his faith, the guy who wants to make money, the guy who wants to spend money without paying taxes, the guy who wants to fondle his gun**, all have a lot in common. **They all want the government to go away.** That is what holds together the conservative movement." He'd later add property-rights nuts and homeschoolers to the list, forming the unhinged core of the new GOP and what would become fertile ground for Tea Party organizing and the weaponization of the crazies.[19]

As the frayed intellectual rationalizations of ever-ballooning tax cuts alongside the gonzo demands of an ever-more-detached-from-reality coalition became strained to *waaaay* beyond the breaking point, the Michelle Bachmann-ization of the GOP was inevitable, as was perhaps the elevation of a former professional wrestling clown and reality show putz to be the party's candidate.

Today's GOP, after three decades of having its intellectual roots poison-gassed while so-called RINOs (Republicans In Name Only) were being strafed, then barrel-bombed, by Christian-Right Jihadists and Tax-Cut-or-Die Baathists, is little more than a smoking ruin of its previous self, an Aleppo-on-the-Potomac—and a party with a single-minded goal: a radicalized suicide-bomber GOP, drugged-up, running wild-eyed, with thumb on trigger and the sole aim of blowing up the FDR and postwar liberal America.

V.
Transnational
Kleptocrats Unite!

"I will, to the best of my Judgment, discharge the duties of the office with that impartiality and zeal for the public good, which ought never to suffer connections of blood or friendship to intermingle, so as to have the least sway on decision of a public nature."

George Washington, Letter to Benjamin Harrison, 1789

Manila Lie

In perhaps one of his most brazen in-your-face fuck yous to the American people and the idea of basic oversight, Donald Trump held a hastily called presser on January 11 to address swirling questions about the almost limitless conflicts of interest his many businesses represented. Piled next to him, carried in dramatically by aides, were unruly stacks of unmarked manila folders, which at one point Trump turned toward saying each contained a different document he'd signed earlier that day relinquishing control of all his business interests to his sons. The folders were nothing more than a prop—blank documents all, as reporters soon discovered—while the presser itself was one more Potemkin stunt to fool critics. [1] "He has all of the conflicts of interest that he had before," said Richard Painter, chief ethics lawyer under George W. Bush, dismissing the presser. "We don't know who his business partners are, we don't know who he owes."[2]

We don't know, in short, whether or not he signed over control of his business empire to Beavis and Butthead.

We do know that one of his central promises, that the Trump organization will not pursue any new foreign deals during the entire period of his presidency, was broken less than a week later with the announced expansion of his Scottish golf course,[3] while Don and Eric have since taken to traveling the world, largely on the taxpayers' tab, investigating and signing new deals.[4] And as to promising to not read any news of what's happening at Trump properties, the Tweetmaster-in-Chief continues to follow, almost exclusively, a whole variety of Trump organization Twitter accounts… of course, he doesn't read them…

"Trump is poised to mingle business and government," predicted David Frum, "with an audacity and on a scale more reminiscent of a leader in a post-Soviet republic than anything ever before seen in the United States."

The broader GOP isn't immune, as power players from across the business world cash in on the Trump bounce. CNBC even compiled a "Trump Cabinet Index," linking prominent members of the administration to companies they're involved in, and discovered that since the election it's considerably outperformed broader market indices.[5]

"The princes of the GOP have elevated business concerns to the level of national interest," writes Richard Cohen. "This accounts for the procession of Wall Street types who have backed Trump almost from the start—Wilbur Ross, Carl Icahn and Steve Schwarzman, who once said of a possible tax increase on private-equity firms:

'It's a war. It's like when Hitler invaded Poland in 1939.'

"In a recent speech at UCLA," he continues, "Bret Stephens, the deputy editorial page editor of the *Wall Street Journal* and an unquestioned conservative, likened the way 'the new Trumpian conservatives have made their peace with their new political master' to those pathetic souls who once found virtue, if not inevitability, in Stalinism. But the billionaires and politicians who sit around Trump's table and chortle cravenly at the boss's jokes do not fear for their lives or their jobs. No Siberia awaits them."[6]

All In the Family

"Nepotism is kind of a factor of life," Eric Trump blithely told *Forbes* in March 2017, while claiming to still be a card-carrying member of the Trump Meritocracy. "You know, if we didn't do a good job, if we weren't competent, believe me, we wouldn't be in this spot."[7] All good kleptocrats love to spread the love, especially to their own families—they need to if they want to build a dynasty. And if it has ambitions to anything, Brand Trump wants to dynastate (I know, there ain't no such verb—but there ain't no Trump Meritocracy either, so there.)

With Eric and Don running the show from the outside in a wink-wink (totally not) blind trust, the inside job goes to Jared Kushner and wife Ivanka. Kushner, who's been appointed Secretary of Everything, is tasked with mending bilateral ties with Mexico, reinventing government from the ground up, solving the nation's opioid crisis, fixing the war in Iraq… and oh yes, forging a peace deal between Israelis and Palestinians.[8]

And Who—Exactly—Is Jared Kushner?

The son of a billionaire (do I have to say it?) real estate developer, and grandson of Holocaust survivors, the "sleek, tall and patrician" Kushner attended Harvard and New York University, and in billionaire-meritocractic style, took over his father's billion-dollar business empire in 2008. Said to be "spookily presentable," he married the president's favorite child, Ivanka, in 2009.[9] A longtime Bloomberg Democrat, Kushner says that it was traveling the nation with Trump during the campaign that forced him out of his Upper West Side "bubble" to finally understand why "thousands of ordinary Americans shouted in fury about government regulations and the Common Core curriculum." Ordinary Americans didn't care about the planet warming. What they wanted were coal mining jobs. As Andrew Rice described it, "The gilded scales fell from his eyes."[10]

But he's qualified or, as Eric says, he "wouldn't be in this spot."

Sure—in the same way many a Greek bureaucrat is qualified these days: by being related to the doofus who won the election.

As political commentator Jason Linkins notes, Kushner comes to D.C. with "no government experience, no policy experience, no diplomatic experience, and business experience limited to his family's real estate development firm, a brief stint as a newspaper publisher, and briefly bidding to acquire the Los Angeles Dodgers."[11] While Elizabeth Spiers, who worked closely with him at the New York *Observer*, worries his new responsibilities reflect nothing but a "a vanity project, one that exists primarily to put Kushner in the same room with people he admires whom he wouldn't have had access to before, glossing government agencies in the process with a thin veneer of what appears to be capitalism but is really just nihilistic cost-cutting designed to project the optics of efficiency."[12]

~~White~~ Russia House Blues

Though like many of Trump's revolving door advisers and staff, especially those he brought with him from the campaign, Jared may not be around long enough to do little more than a few tone-deaf, flak-jacketed photo-ops in the Iraqi sun. Late in May, reports surfaced that Kushner personally asked Sergey Kislyak, Russia's ambassador to the United States, to set up secret, back-channel communications, out of the Russian embassies in D.C. and New York, for the incoming Trump team to be able to communicate in private with their Russian counterparts and others in Moscow. The revelation has lifted Kushner's star in the FBI's book: he's now one more focus of their investigation into ties between the Trump campaign and Putin's regime.[13]

But so far it's all OK, because Donald says so.[14]

"I like nepotism." Trump told CNN's Larry King in 2007. "I think, you know, a lot of people say 'Oh, nepotism.' Usually these are people without children. But I like nepotism."

VI.
Autocracy Now

"In time of actual war, great discretionary powers are constantly given to the Executive Magistrate. Constant apprehension of War, has the same tendency to render the head too large for the body. A standing military force, with an overgrown Executive will not long be safe companions to liberty. The means of defence agst. foreign danger, have been always the instruments of tyranny at home. Among the Romans it was a standing maxim to excite a war, whenever a revolt was apprehended. Throughout all Europe, the armies kept up under the pretext of defending, have enslaved the people."

James Madison, Speech, Constitutional Convention, 1787

"How to Build an Autocracy"

... or so conservative columnist David Frum titled his long-form and deeply thought essay, published days after Donald Trump's inauguration, which paints a measured yet unsettling portrait of an America subtly coming apart at the seams over the coming years of a Trump administration. Frum is no bomb-throwing alarmist, and the vision that emerges is of a spreading kleptocracy, where journalists, corporations, and citizens learn that it's in their best interest not to question too much or dig too deeply into the widening web of Trump-branded or Trump-linked organizations that seem to daily suck more and more from the collective public teat.

"A would-be kleptocrat is actually better served by spreading cynicism than by deceiving followers with false beliefs:

Believers can be disillusioned; people who expect to hear only lies can hardly complain when a lie is exposed."

Guns and bunkers won't help you either, nor will they hold back the rise of Trumpistan. "Those citizens who fantasize about defying tyranny from within fortified compounds," he concludes, "have never understood how liberty is actually threatened in a modern bureaucratic state: not by diktat and violence, but by the slow, demoralizing process of corruption and deceit."

Or when cable news channel RT or website *Sputnik News*—both Russian state propaganda arms—are as trusted or distrusted as the *New York Times* or *Washington Post,* an argument Trump is actively pushing, it's the nihilists who rule given power by the gaping chasm of public cynicism.[1]

"Failing @NYTimes"

Calling respected news outlets like CNN and the *New York Times* "FAKE NEWS!" "failing" and "Enemy of the American people!"—as he tweeted, echoing, according to the same Gray Lady that Trump denounced, an all-purpose attack phrase projectile-vomited by autocrats since the French Revolution, and one that often led to the brutal killing of the target—Trump follows in the timeworn goosesteps of many an insecure tyrant-in-training-wheels before him.[2]

It's a two-fold strategy: first to delegitimize trusted sources of information and then to build an alternative media universe—a network of fake news and propaganda outlets that constantly reinforce each other while undermining broader public trust and spreading cynicism.[3]

Steve Bannon's recent breezy put-down of the media as "the opposition party" as he passed them in a White House hall is, even he admits, only the beginning. Bannon promised to raise the heat daily: "It's going to get worse every day for the media," he threatened,[4] while Trump adviser and former reality TV star Omarosa Manigault openly bullied and "physically intimidated" reporter April Ryan, making verbal threats and claiming Ryan was one of many journalists on whom Trump officials had collected 'dossiers' of damning intel.[5]

Trump's not been shy about directly citing right-wing or conspiracy news sites like One America News Network or *Infowars* to back up his own tweeted paranoia, or only calling on conservative news outlets like the *Daily Caller, Christian Broadcasting News* and Townhall.com, as he did for several consecutive press conferences.[6] Add to that the White House press credentials given to alt-right blogger for *The Gateway Pundit,* and also founder of "Twinks4Trump," Lucian Wintrich, who commemorated the occasion by posting a selfie from the press room podium flashing a "white power" hand signal along with a Pepe the Frog emoji.[7] Ari Fleischer, Dubya's former press secretary, advises Trump to withhold credentials from outlets it deems "too liberal or unfair."[8] And throw in that Russian propaganda arms *Sputnik News* and RT applied for White House press credentials,[9] while the since defenestrated Sean Spicer had taken to sidelining members of the press the administration is angry with in postbriefing press gaggles,[10] and you have the beginnings of the creation of the Alternative Media Universe. And not just with the aim of shifting the press narrative into the breathless cries of the right wing fever dream or filling the media echo chamber with post-truth non-facts, but because, as Russian-born journalist Masha Gessen writes on Trump's affinity with Putin:

"Lying is the message...

... It's not just that both Putin and Trump lie, it is that they lie in the same way and for the same purpose: blatantly, to assert power over truth itself."[11]

"In a society where few people walk to work," David Frum expands, "why mobilize young men in matching shirts to command the streets?

If you're seeking to domineer and bully, you want your storm troopers to go online, where the more important traffic is. Demagogues need no longer stand erect for hours orating into a radio microphone. Tweet lies from a smartphone instead."[12] With power over truth, or the ability, as Kellyanne Conway says, to conjure "alternative facts" out of thin air, our would-be autocrat-in-chief is proving his ability to dominate reality itself, and not only over his lackeys, but over a large segment of the electorate.

"I don't ever want to call a court biased…"

But Trump did, declaring an all-guns-blazing war on the judiciary—launching laser-guided tweets targeting Ninth Circuit Federal Court Judge James Robart for blocking his hastily, and let's face it, hand-crayoned executive order travel ban for seven Muslim-majority nations. "**The opinion of this so-called judge**," Trump rage-tweeted on a Saturday afternoon—*sans* the reputedly mollifying influence of Orthodox Jewish son-in-law Jared Kushner, away observing Sabbath, "which essentially takes law-enforcement away from our country, is ridiculous and will be overturned!" Unable to contain his toddler's outraged id, nor sideline his anger for cooler reflection, he upped the ante the following day, this time not bothering to mask the scent of threat, "Just cannot believe a judge would put our country in such peril. **If something happens blame him and court system.** People pouring in. Bad!"[13]

The more-than-implied threat was taken a little too literally by some of his more militant dittoheads, who took up their master's voice and put it into their own, less-varnished words—prompting federal and local law enforcement agencies to temporarily increase security protection, citing the safety of several of Ninth Circuit judges.[14] *Still* unable to send his inner toddler to the naughty step, days later Trump "sneered" to a meeting of police chiefs, "A bad high school student would understand this," he said, and added, "I don't ever want to call a court biased and we haven't had a decision yet. But courts seem to be so political, and it would be so great for our justice system if they would be able to read a statement and do what's right ... I have to be honest that if these judges wanted to, in my opinion, help the court in terms of respect for the court, they'd do what they should be doing. It's so sad."[15]

Recall, this was the candidate who said...[16]

"I will be so presidential, you will be so bored."

He'd been here many times in the middle of the presidential campaign, vehemently attacking Mexican American Judge Gonzalo Curiel's heritage as a "conflict of interest" and that as a result he was "giving us very unfair rulings" over the potential release of records in a Trump University fraud case.[17] Judge Curiel would rule in Trump's favor, something that George Shepherd argued ironically, "may have played a crucial role in clearing the way for Trump's election. If the trial had occurred as originally scheduled, Trump would have been forced to defend against charges that he defrauded thousands of people during the height of the presidential campaign."[18]

Because Who Questions the President...?

Stephen Miller, Trump's just-out-of-diaper's NatSec adviser, chose to go nuclear on the justice system, saying, "I think that it's been an important reminder to all Americans that we have a judiciary that has taken far too much power and become, in many cases, a supreme branch of government. One unelected judge in Seattle cannot remake laws for the entire country. I mean this is just crazy, the idea that you have a judge in Seattle say that a foreign national living in Libya has an effective right to enter the United States is beyond anything we've ever seen before. **The end result of this, though, is that our opponents, the media and the whole world will soon see as we begin to take further actions, that the powers of the president to protect our country are very substantial and will not be questioned."[19]**

Setting the Stage for an Attack?

... or so former Assistant Attorney General and Harvard Law School Professor Jack Goldsmith speculates: "the only reason I can think of is that Trump is setting the scene to blame judges after an attack that has any conceivable connection to immigration ... If Trump assumes that there will be a bad terrorist attack on his watch, blaming judges now will deflect blame and enhance his power more than usual after the next attack." Law and politics writer Dahlia Lithwick pulls no punches, writing, "I continue to believe that his attacks on the judicial branch are deliberately destabilizing for their own sake and that they are deliberately politicizing a branch of government ... **because Trump and Steve Bannon want to delegitimize the court system.**"[20]

Or Maybe Plain Old Ass-Covering?

... because why stop with the judges when you can prevent experienced prosecutors from opening investigations, or scuttle ones that might already be underway. Which is what the March 10 "firing" of *all* current US Attorneys sure looked like. They weren't actually fired, but good as, so the *New York Times* reported, with immediate letters of resignation demanded and that their desks be cleared by midnight. It's not unusual for incoming administrations to fire previous US Attorneys, but the suddenness, the zero notice given, while no replacements were lined up to fill the vacancies, make this "firing" unprecedented.[21] "I do believe that something odd happened," Norm Eisen, a former White House ethics lawyer, said. "You don't decide to keep 46 folks on, then suddenly demand their immediate exit, without some precipitating cause or causes."[22]

Oh yes, only two days before, three prominent independent watchdog groups sent a letter to Obama-appointed US Attorney Preet Bharara to investigate questions around President Trump and payments or other benefits from foreign governments through his business interests in violation the Constitution's emoluments clause. The letter argued that Trump's continued failure to fully divest himself of his myriad business interests put him in serious legal hazard of being in violation of the Constitution.[23]

Not Exactly a Pair of Lead Boots, but...

That they picked Bharara to go after Trump was no coincidence—described as "the man who terrifies Wall Street" and someone who has waged a successful, and deeply nonpartisan, campaign to attack New York state corruption in both the Republican and Democratic parties, he was an ideal choice to go after alleged administration violations or wrongdoing.[24] Rep. Elijah Cummings raised the possible connection between the firing and investigations into President Trump.[25] In letting him go, one thing's for sure, Trump (temporarily) inoculates himself against a significant source of legal jeopardy.

VII.
Voodoo to Voldemort

"When a man unprincipled in private life desperate in his fortune, bold in his temper, possessed of considerable talents, having the advantage of military habits—despotic in his ordinary demeanour—known to have scoffed in private at the principles of liberty—when such a man is seen to mount the hobby horse of popularity—to join in the cry of danger to liberty—to take every opportunity of embarrassing the General Government & bringing it under suspicion—to flatter and fall in with all the non sense of the zealots of the day—It may justly be suspected that his object is to throw things into confusion that he may 'ride the storm and direct the whirlwind.'"

Alexander Hamilton,
Objections and Answers Respecting the Administration, 1792

"They're bringing drugs. They're bringing crime. They're rapists..."

No one builds a good ol' ass-kickin' autocracy without finding someone to punch. On the campaign trail Trump learned how to be a master bully—picking on Mexicans (as the above Trump rally quote illustrates), immigrants, Muslims, shady "globalists," the physically disabled, liberals, elites, journalists, and pretty much any woman who didn't live up to his teenage-boy photoshopped bedroom poster idea of beauty. But no budding autocrat gets to sew on his Cruelty To General Humanity Badge until he... well... proves he can cruelly turn his own citizens against each other. Or in the case of Donald Trump, until he can show that...

"Ordinary Americans Carried Out Inhumane Acts..."

... as author Chris Edelson writes, describing the impact of the *first hours* of Trump's executive order banning travel from several Muslim-majority nations. "A week ago, men and women went to work at airports around the United States as they always do. They showered, got dressed, ate breakfast, perhaps dropped off their kids at school. Then they reported to their jobs as federal government employees, where, according to news reports, one of them handcuffed a 5-year-old child, separated him from his mother and detained him alone for several hours at Dulles airport." Multiply this scene hundreds of times on a single day, then multiply that by years, and you arrive at the basic arithmetic of Trump-fueled hate. Robert Reich expands over at *Salon*, arguing that "Trump is forcing Americans to participate in an orgy of unnecessary cruelty."[1]

"Deportation Force"

Describing a pair of memos issued by then homeland security secretary John Kelly, the *New York Times* writes, "They are the battle plan for the 'deportation force' President Trump promised in the campaign... [and] remarkable for... how they seek to make the deportation machinery more extreme and frightening (and expensive), to the detriment of deeply held American values... **[Kelly] makes practically every deportable person a deportation priority**... Proportionality, discretion, the idea that some convictions are unjust, the principles behind criminal-justice reform—these concepts do not apply. The targets now don't even have to be criminals. They could simply have been accused of a crime (that is, still presumed 'innocent') or have done something that makes an immigration agent believe that they might possibly face charges."[2]

Echoes of Nazi Germany

The newly formed Victims Of Immigration Crime Engagement Office, or VOICE, lists weekly crimes committed by immigrants—a fear-mongering campaign with only one purpose: to further alienate the public against undocumented immigrants and provide cover for senseless acts of cruelty carried out in the name of border enforcement. "An expert on concentration camps has already pointed out," writes Daniel Camacho, "that the weekly list of crimes bears deeply troubling resemblances to Nazi–era Germany, where Hitler published Jewish crimes."[3]

A New American Cruelty...

... made easy, as Sarah Kenzidor tells is, by Trump's affinity to "divide people between haters and losers, a cheap shot that is actually a fairly useful way to categorize his own team. Haters, or string-pullers, include people like Roger Stone, Paul Manafort, and Steve Bannon... Fellow bigots—racist Jeff Sessions, [since jettisoned] Islamophobic Michael Flynn—fit the 'haters' mold: powerful players who disregard constitutional principles in order to force a narrow and cruel vision of America into practice. The losers comprise the bulk of Trump's cabinet appointees, who have each been assigned an institution about which they either know nothing, actively want to destroy, or both."[4]

While Stoking Violence Only Strengthens Trump...

... as David Frum points out, arguing that civil unrest "will be a resource" and that rather than repressing it, he'll want to "publicize it"— the more offensive the better. "Calculated outrage is an old political trick," he reminds us, "but nobody in the history of American politics has deployed it as aggressively, as repeatedly, or with such success as Donald Trump. **If there is harsh law enforcement by the Trump administration, it will benefit the president not to the extent that it quashes unrest, but to the extent that it enflames more of it, ratifying the apocalyptic vision that haunted his speech at the convention."**[5]

"The grotesque, frowning, sleepy eyed, out of shape, swamp dweller, peeing...

"... with his pants pulled down because-it-feels-good-man frog *is an ideology*, one which steers into the skid of its own patheticness," or so Dale Beran puts it, describing Pepe the Frog, the coded mascot of the alt-right.

"Pepe symbolizes embracing your loserdom, owning it," Beran writes. "It is, in other words, a value system, one reveling in deplorableness and being pridefully dispossessed. It is a culture of hopelessness, of knowing 'the system is rigged.'"[6]

Or welcome to…

Victims'R'Us™

… the rapidly expanding one-stop big box GOP ideology store that's been popping up all over Red State America these past couple of decades, sucking the life out of locally sourced, free range voices and strangling old-school conservative mom and pop beliefs that for decades kept small-town political life thriving.

Like Pepe, the smirking loser with attitude, much of the GOP base has come to revel in its self-image as perennial victim, Charlie Brown in an endlessly looping GIF trying to kick that football while simultaneously scorning the opposition "as #triggered snowflakes who need a 'safe space,'" as policy analyst Sean McElwee describes. "In the words of Trump's chief strategist Stephen Bannon, '**They're either a victim of race. They're victim of their sexual preference. They're a victim of gender. All about victimhood and the United States is the great oppressor, not the great liberator.'**"[7]

Trumpism was ignited in its own cauldron of self-loathing and loathing glee. No doubt many who listened to Trump's bordering-on-the-deranged campaign rants, those sock-you-in-the-face stem-winders where his rising decibel-level became the only argument, recognized in themselves either abuser or victim, perhaps both, unable to turn away from the horror-show mirror or the horror-show life.

"Trumpism is a movement built on victimhood," argues John Paul Brammer. "It holds that Americans are unemployed because immigrants stole their jobs. It argues that people of color are diluting the culture of America and that LGBT people having rights is an attack on the traditional family. Its slogan, Make America Great Again, speaks to that victimhood. We were great once. We aren't anymore, because of *those* people."[8]

Voldemort Economics

How do we get from Ronald Reagan's soaring vision of the "shining city on the hill" to Donald Trump's apocalypse-smeared lenses as he looks out across a ruination of American carnage? Maybe go back to the Gipper himself, and an ideology that was already peeling away from any broadly recognized notion of reason and crumbling into absurdities at his feet. The internal logical dissonance of Reagan's "Voodoo economics"—that massive tax cuts along with exploding military spending *reduce* the deficit—might well be the original sin of modern conservative thought.

There's method to the hoodoo: unshackled from burdensome taxes, the economic, creative and "animal" spirits of the American people are unleashed, conjuring a previously unimagined expansion of the US economy. Practice has again and again proved otherwise, but this has not stopped GOP ideologues from doubling, tripling, and quadrupling down—resulting in a party establishment that at its foundations needs to rationalize increasingly divorced-from-reality policy proposals and therefore cultivate an ever-more-polarized base and persuade them more often than not that black is white and 2 plus 2 equals 5—or 3 or 7 or 1—just anything but 4.

Donald Trump's tortured revivification of the voodoo economics zombie, the most extreme and magical yet, has him waving Draco Malfoy's 10-inch hawthorn wand, embedded with, you guessed it, a single unicorn hair, at any number of CEOs, corporations, and industries, demanding they bring back jobs from overseas and rebuild the sepia-toned industrial fairy land of the 1950s. **With all the bullying bluster, the whiplash policy proposals that has Trump appearing and disappearing simultaneously from multiple points of view while seeming to hover in a terrifying miasmic fog over all, and his** obvious belief that all he needs is to chant the right words for the economy to explode, what else to call it but "Voldemort economics."

Which leads us to the inevitable question when it comes to a reality-averse GOP:

Is that a banana in your pants, or are you just happy to see me?

If you're not a walkin' talkin' tax cut for the ultra rich, and it's the GOP or any of their cronies you're talking to, it's pretty much a sure bet these days to be a banana. From the paranoid banshee-cries of 1980s talk radio to Rush Limbaugh and his Dittoheads in the 1990s and the suffocating, ideologically-pure bear hug of Fox News in the Bush and Obama eras, the US media landscape has seen a vast tilt rightward while these same news outlets let out a primal scream of accusation, claiming the opposite has in fact been happening. A neat strategy, and one that worked: uber-biased media naming and shaming their ideological "enemies" as biased-to-the-max, pulling them into the maelstrom that is contemporary right-wing nuttery and self-deception.

The year 2016 strapped on rockets mounted with afterburners and sent these trends to farcically absurd new heights with the spread of "fake news"—wholly fabricated stories carefully designed to spark indignation, more often on the right but sometimes on the left, and what journalist Nick Bilton described as **"perhaps the most significant digital epidemic facing the media, government, and, at the risk of sounding mildly hysterical, democracy itself."**[9] Hillary Clinton bore much of the brunt—stories painting her as a pathological liar, murderer, serial lesbian, child rapist, and madam of a high-class pedophile ring run out of the back room of a DC pizza joint caught fire on social media and internet memes on the fringes of the far right *and* left (here's looking at you, Bernie Bros and Jill Stein goose-steppers), and further confused the befuddled middle.

Blurring the lines "between the imaginary and real world," as writer Walter Kirn described it, **fake news is designed to dramatically undermine trust in traditional forms of media. "In an age where there are few authorities," Kirn said, "where the** *New York Times* **no longer sits atop the journalistic pyramid, the question of where to look for real stories and truthful accounts of life is a huge one.** Being an American is all about dealing with BS artists, with promotion and marketing. In that world of deception, in which our economy almost runs on deception—call it advertising—you have a huge, unaddressed appetite for truth… We live in a bizarre, topsy-turvy universe of statements whose value we can't really assess, whose truths we can't really grade, and once again how to orient yourself when lost seems to me to be the great American problem. We're more lost than ever."[10]

Junkies on the Outrage Treadmill

The narrative of victimhood that's taken much of the GOP by the throat and the flu-like spread of fake news, clickbait and hyperpartisan websites are inextricably linked: both demand each other to survive, and both strengthen each other in a self-perpetuating feedback loop. The confluence of technology with the ballooning internal contradictions and delusions of right wing policy "solutions" peddled these days by the GOP pretty much assures that if we didn't already have fake news, they would have had to invent it. How else to keep slipping a large segment of their base the opium of perennial confusion over what's actually happened over the last eight years, the real-world implications of their policies, and where their genuine interests lie (hint: it ain't blue collar America)?

The left's far from immune, as outrage, the bitcoin currency that's mined not only for clicks, but real dollars, is alive and well on all sides in post-Obama America. The unchecked spread of false memes and "a friend of a friend told me…" stories on Facebook—like fake reports of ICE checkpoints or raids in New York City subway cars[11]—do little more than terrify already victimized populations while offering up the equally fake balm of "doing something good" for the tender egos of largely white liberal "like" button jockeys.

Thus it is in the ever meowing…

Cat Video Industrial Complex

… which many on the alt-right have bigly plans for, such as the formation of "'culture tanks' to produce movies that make anti-immigrant conservatism look cool and advocacy arms that resemble *BuzzFeed* more than The Heritage Foundation. **They talk elliptically about internet memes replacing white papers as the currency of the policy realm, pushed out by 'social media strike forces' trained in the ways of fourth-generation, insurgency-style warfare."**[12]

Facts just get in the way…

… as Tristran Bridges tells us. "Whether it's about the size of his inauguration crowd, patently false and fear-mongering inaccuracies about transgender persons in bathrooms, rates of violent crime in the U.S., or anything else, lately it feels like the facts don't seem to matter." He blames what social scientists call the *backfire effect*.

"**As a rule, misinformed people do not change their minds once they have been presented with facts that challenge their beliefs. But, beyond simply not changing their minds when they should, research shows that they are likely to become *more* attached to their mistaken beliefs.**"[13] While the social capital that fake news gives us cements us to our peers. "Spreading a tall tale also gives people something even more important than false expertise—it lets them know who's on their side."[14]

The shape of fakery to come

Rapid advancements in both audio and video technology will soon make possible the seamless creation of fake audio and video clips on a home desktop that are genuinely indistinguishable from real ones. Imagine a viral video of Hillary Clinton admitting to an affair with former aide and suicide Vince Foster, who right wing nutjobs believe she killed, or one of Trump happily yukking it up about his sexual exploits in Moscow—both will soon be handily DIY and equally difficult to verify or prove false. By the 2018 midterms, and certainly by the 2020 general election, warns Bilton:

"There will not only be thousands of fake-news articles floating around the Internet, but also countless fake videos and fake audio clips, too."[15]

VIII.
Putin Picks His "Idiot"

"A nation which can prefer disgrace to danger is prepared for a master, and deserves one."

Alexander Hamilton, The Warning No. III, 1797

"Buyer's Remorse..."

... or what fake news giveth, fake news taketh away

The buyer in this case being Vladimir Putin, Russia's often bare-chested, tiger-wrastling Bro-tocrat, who thought he found a bro-mate in the over-the-top brawling incoherence of The Donald. If the so-called "dossier" is to be believed—the folder of highly sensitive opposition research compiled by former UK spy Christopher Steele for an unknown US political candidate—Putin's regrets started early, in August 2016, when top Kremlin aides began to seriously doubt the mental stability of the horse they'd bet the farm on.[1] What took them so long? Maybe it was having Putin—a happy-go-lucky "terror sponsor," as Garry Kasparov calls him,[2] and journalist and political opponent-murdering kleptocrat who's running a whole nation as little more than a personal piggy bank for himself and his multibillionaire wolf pack buddies—as their model for upstanding citizen of the year.

Dropping publically weeks *after* the election, the dossier made explosive allegations against Trump and his aides—not least of which was the dubious claim of a notorious Donald Trump/multiple prostitute piss orgy on a Moscow bed Barack and Michelle Obama once shared. But by February, top intelligence officers had begun to corroborate parts of the dossier's less urine-soaked claims, lending "greater confidence" to other, as yet unverified, allegations.[3] Trump, who calls shaking hands "barbaric," laughed off the claims, saying, "I'm also very much of a germaphobe, by the way, believe me."[4]

The gist was simple: a broad conspiracy existed between Donald Trump's campaign and the Kremlin that in exchange for lifting US sanctions on Russia and softening the US stance to the Russian invasion of Ukraine, the Kremlin would coordinate attacks and attempts to discredit Hillary Clinton through fake news outlets, hacking of email accounts and the selective release of hacked documents to Russia-financed Twitter trolls and the one-time self-proclaimed champion of freedom of information, WikiLeaks. Trump himself was accused of paying some of the Russian trolls through intermediaries.[5]

The details are considerably messier. In the months since, a genuinely Escher-like web of interconnections has emerged tying close Trump associates to Mother Russia, while the Ghost of Russia's Past continues to haunt Trump himself. In 2008, the president's son Don Jr. proudly claimed, **"Russians make up a pretty disproportionate cross-section of a lot of our assets... We see a lot of money pouring in from Russia."** What exactly he was referring to he never made clear. Big Daddy Trump insists, in tweets and interviews, that he has no financial interest in Russia whatsoever, calling the allegations, in his characteristic all-caps bombast, "FAKE NEWS!"[6]

Of course, there's no *evidence*... oh wait... isn't that a smoking gun in your hand?

Actually—as the Brits say—the ONLY change the Trump campaign demanded to the Republican Party platform at the July 2016 national convention was to soften language on the US approach to Russia's invasion of Ukraine.[7] What we didn't know then, but know now, was that several Trump campaign aides and staffers met with Russian Ambassador Sergey Kislyak that same week—including current Attorney General Jeff Sessions along with two members of Trump's national security advisory committee, Carter Page and J.D. Gordon.[8]

"That money we have is blood money."

Trump's revolving door campaign manager at the time, Paul Manafort, was already under a cloud for past lobbying work for Ukraine's pro-Russian President Viktor Yanukovych, who was deposed in 2014 for gold-plaited toilet levels of corruption and forced to make a midnight run to Moscow.

The grandson of Italian immigrants, Manafort is a lifelong Connecticut Republican who, like Trump, grew up in a wealthy real estate family, but chose to go into politics, starting after a Georgetown education when he became an adviser to Gerald Ford's 1976 campaign. With a reputation of "deep and sometimes murky, connections in Washington and around the world," he has helped rehabilitate the tarnished images of dictators like the Congo's Mobutu Sese Seko and Ferdinand Marcos of the Philippines in the eyes of the American people.[9] *Slate*'s Franklin Foer called this Manafort's special gift. "He would recast them as noble heroes—venerated by Washington think tanks, deluged with money from Congress."[10] How did he land the primo job with Team Trump? The answer, like Manafort himself, is murky, with the *New York Times* writing, "Through family and friends, handshakes and hyperbole,"[11] while others argue there's good evidence he deliberately maneuvered himself into the position.[12]

In hacked texts, Manafort's daughter, Andrea Manafort, had long been uneasy about her father's work—both for Ukraine and later for Donald Trump. "Don't fool yourself," she wrote to her sister in 2015. "That money we have is blood money." In another she described her dad and Trump as a "perfect pair" of "power-hungry egomaniacs."[13] Most chillingly, referencing the deaths of protestors in Kiev in 2014, she wrote, "You know he has killed people in Ukraine? Knowingly.

As a tactic to outrage the world and get focus on Ukraine. Remember when there were all those deaths taking place. A while back. About a year ago. Revolts and what not. Do you know whose strategy that was to cause that, to send those people out and get them slaughtered."[14]

The stories of a Russia connection caught up with him weeks after the Republican Convention, and he was let go in what Trump insiders insisted was a routine campaign shake-up. "I am very appreciative for his great work in helping to get us where we are today," Donald Trump said in a statement, "and in particular his work guiding us through the delegate and convention process. **Paul is a true professional and I wish him the greatest success.**"[15]

Well—the greatest success, maybe, but not so much the kick out the door, as Andrea texted to a friend days after, writing, "So I got to the bottom of it, as I suspected my dad resigned from being the public face of the campaign. But is still very much involved behind the scenes."[16]

But hey…

… it's not like he was secretly being PAID…

… ten million dollars a year…

… to promote a vast plan to aid Russian interests…

… and benefit the Putin regime…

… or…?

In March 2017, the *Associated Press* reported that in fact he was getting paid—**ten million dollars a year** *since 2006*—by a Russian oligarch and close ally of Vladimir Putin, to promote Russian interests in the West. "According to documents that we've reviewed, Paul Manafort secretly worked for a Russian oligarch who wanted him to promote Russian interests," the AP's Chad Day told NPR. "And in particular, he wrote a memo that outlined this kind of vast plan for him to promote Russian interests in the former Soviet republics—and also to specifically benefit the Putin government."[17] The full AP report was considerably more damning, claiming, "Manafort proposed... that he would **influence politics, business dealings and news coverage inside the United States,** Europe and the former Soviet republics to benefit the Putin government."[18]

But he was just a volunteer...

... said the administration who ran from him like he was a house on fire after the news broke—someone "who played a very limited role for a very limited amount of time."[19] While true that Manafort was not being paid by the Trump campaign (why would he, he was raking in ludicrous sums of money elsewhere), the claim of a limited role is laughable for a man who was campaign manager and chief strategist in Trump's renowned bare-bones operation for half of 2016... and for much longer, if Andrea Manafort is right.

Which brings us to the...

... the Brief, Unhappy Tenure of Mike Flynn

Another Putin apparatchik who fell afoul of being... well... another Putin apparatchik... A former director of the Defense Intelligence Agency under Obama, he was originally forced out, according to Colin Powell in a hacked e-mail reported by the *Washington Post*, for being someone who was "abusive with staff, didn't listen, worked against policy, bad management, etc." The *New York Times* characterized him as having a "loose relationship with facts," noting he "has said that Shariah, or Islamic law, is spreading in the United States (it is not). His dubious assertions are so common that when he ran the Defense Intelligence Agency, subordinates came up with a name for the phenomenon: They called them 'Flynn facts.'"[20]

Dubbed "America's angriest general"—it was a genuinely unhinged Flynn who led a snarling, screaming, out-for-blood mob—otherwise known as delegates at the Republican National Convention in Cleveland—in a burn-the-house-down Hillary-roasting floor-thumper of a chant with...[21]

"LOCK HER UP! YES, THAT'S RIGHT, *LOCK HER UP!*"

So how does someone become the shortest serving National Security Adviser in the post's history?

Feeling the burn of Obama's firing—he had quickly become one of Obama's most vociferous foreign policy critics, regularly appearing on Fox News to blast the president—Flynn turned to the one man in the world who not only shared his violently Islamophobic views, but also had the power to do something about it: Vladimir Putin. By December 2015, he was sitting elbow to elbow with the man himself as a guest of honor at a Moscow gala dinner, along with Green Party candidate Jill Stein and a host of serious Kremlin and Russian power players.[22] Referring to this dinner, the dossier says efforts to cultivate these figures had been "successful in terms of perceived outcomes." The outcome in this case is the allegation that the Trump campaign agreed to "raise defense commitments in the Baltics and Eastern Europe to deflect attention away from Ukraine."[23]

An early yapping bulldog in Trump's corner when much of the Republican national security establishment was throwing serious shade in Orangehead's direction, Flynn found a potential bro-in-chief in Trump and his seeming Islam-hate. **"Islamist militancy poses an existential threat on a global scale, and the Muslim faith itself is the source of the problem, [Flynn] said**, describing it as a political ideology, not a religion. He has even at times gone so far as to call it a political ideology that has 'metastasized' into a 'malignant cancer.'"[24] His elevation to National Security Adviser sent a blinding flare through NatSec circles that one of Trump's campaign trail whipping boys, "radical Islamic terror," would take center stage in foreign policy decision-making along with a softening of the US stance toward Russia. By mid-January, Trump was open to lifting sanctions. "If you get along and if Russia is really helping us," he said…

> **"… why would anybody have sanctions if somebody's doing some really great things?"**[25]

That same week, news broke that earlier, in December, Mike Flynn made a phone call to Russian Ambassador Sergey Kislyak ("one of the top spies" says CNN, "and spy-recruiters in Washington"[26]) on the same day President Obama announced new sanctions on Russia in response to their coordinated disinformation, fake news and email-hacking effort to undermine the 2016 presidential election.[27]

The usual Kremlin tit-for-tat expulsion of American diplomats dating back to the early days of the Cold War, etc. never happened, and Putin took, for the *first time* in such disputes, the high road. Trump congratulated him on Twitter, and also took the unprecedented step for a president-elect of attacking the sitting president in an international dispute. *Reuters* soon upped the tally to five contacts between Flynn and Kislyak on that one day, all of which Flynn insisted were nothing more than pleasantries and making arrangements for a Trump-Putin phone call after inauguration day.[28] He even trotted out Vice President Mike Pence to run cover for him, who appeared on *Face the Nation* and dutifully said Flynn had assured him he never discussed sanctions with the Russian ambassador on the very day that everyone—*everyone!*—else in Washington was talking about nothing else.[29]

The lies collapsed—they tend to when the person you're calling is one of the "top spies" in Washington and, *inconceivable* that Flynn didn't know, whose communications were being actively monitored—and multiple stories circulated that Flynn did in fact discuss sanctions with Kislyak. Surprise, surprise, there were TRANSCRIPTS! At *Newsweek*, Kurt Eichenwald ventured into the thorniest of national security weeds (we're talking RAGTIME-B vs. RAGTIME-C surveillance program protocols) to convincingly argue that for Flynn's side of the conversation to be saved (under almost all circumstances it's a crime to monitor a US citizen without a warrant) and be passed again and again up the chain of command, it would have to have convinced multiple levels of ever higher echelons of the US security apparatus that he was potentially involved in a security breach or crime of devastating proportions.[30]

What he said, what he offered, what he asked for, remains a mystery to the rest of us. Trump's response is the real mystery—he continued to defend Flynn, even when he fired him, a man who had lied to his vice president. Trump had actually—those Brits again—been briefed on Flynn's lies eleven days earlier, yet never told Pence he'd been lied to.

So did Flynn—career military with the chain of command etched into his DNA—go rogue? Lying to Trump, Pence, the whole transition team? Or did Trump clear the calls—explicitly or otherwise—and clandestinely undermine the foreign policy of a sitting president—and his own veep? The latter seems far more likely, especially in an administration where…

Trump's own Putin-shaped boner is one he's never been shy of advertising.

"There has always been a sympathetic authoritarian chord between the Republican presidential nominee and the Russian president," writes George Mason University scholar Michael V. Hayden.[31] "Both are on record as admiring The Strong Leader. They've even complimented one another on the trait. Putin could have been humming along when Trump was claiming 'I alone can fix it' during his acceptance speech at the Republican National Convention." Putin's KGB-tinted lenses, Hayden argues, has him seeing *the other*—any other—as a threat to Russian order, "something to be feared and ultimately crushed." It's a trait Trump shares in his blistering vision of "a corrupt media, international banks, unrestricted immigrants, a variety of globalists, free-traders and (at least some) Muslims."[32]

Trump went so far as to defend Putin's habit of killing journalists and members of the opposition in an interview with Bill O'Reilly, saying, "There's a lot of killers. We've got a lot of killers. What do you think— our country's so innocent."[33]

"Follow the trail of dead Russians…"

… said Clinton Watts, of the Center for Cyber and Homeland Security at George Washington University, on the first day of the Senate Intelligence Committee investigation into Russian hacking of the US election.[34] As many as nine prominent Russians have either been murdered or died under highly suspicious circumstances since the news of Trump's possible ties to Russia exploded in the media. Many of the dead Russians were tied directly to the unverified "dossier"—while others were top-level security officials with access to deep state secrets.[35]

Polezni Durak

So what is Donald Trump?

Manchurian candidate? Self-dealing traitor? Rube of forces beyond his control? Victim of a vast left-wing media conspiracy? Or a regular Joe billionaire simply looking to earn his silver lapel pin in the Transnational Kleptocrat Club?

The most likely, plucking a term from old Soviet KGB-speak, is a *polezni durak*, argues Michael Hayden,[36] which roughly translates to *useful fool*:

"Some naif, manipulated by Moscow, secretly held in contempt, but whose blind support is happily accepted and exploited.

IX.
Count Your Holy Wars

"Remember, democracy never lasts long. It soon wastes, exhausts, and murders itself. There never was a democracy yet that did not commit suicide."

John Adams, Letter to John Taylor, 1814

"We're going to have to do things that we never did before..."

... Donald Trump told *Yahoo News*, reacting to the November 2015 coordinated terrorist attacks in Paris. "And certain things will be done that we never thought would happen in this country in terms of information and learning about the enemy. And so **we're going to have to do certain things that were frankly unthinkable** a year ago."[1]

Unthinkable

Among the "unthinkable" was almost certainly torture, the mandatory registration of Muslims, the murder of families of suspected terrorists, and the carpet bombing of ISIS-controlled cities, regardless of civilian casualties—all of which he advocated on the campaign trail. "Does torture work?" he asked on ABC News, describing conversations with top generals. "And the answer was yes. Absolutely."[2] Later, he'd soften, citing the influence of James "Mad Dog" Mattis, his defense secretary, saying "Mad Dog" would override him on such decisions. It didn't change his mind, he told CNN. *He* still believed torture worked.[3]

General Derangement

Trump makes no secret of his fetish for generals and for what he cites as their brutality, and has appointed them liberally, more than any other modern president, to positions of power across the civilian government. At a South Carolina rally, he repeated a debunked story about General John Pershing in the Philippines, who was said to have captured 50 Muslim prisoners.

"And he lined up the 50 people and they shot 49 of those 50 people, and he said to the 50th, you go back to your people and you tell them what happened—and in 25 years there wasn't a problem."[4]

Blood and Borders

It's nativist nationalism that Donald Trump has always, and pretty much only, been about—and the cruel bombast of terrorizing our enemies that was the cornerstone of his appeal to much of the electorate. An America unleashed, no longer strait-jacketed by the bureaucratic dictates of international treaties or endlessly second-guessed by pinhead lawyers on the battlefield—the comic-book superhero appeal of "see an enemy, punch first and ask questions later" approach which had jacked-up fans doing just that at his rallies.

Trump's nativist primal scream, his blood-and-guts call for American renewal, dovetailed alarmingly with Steve Bannon's vision of America as a warring ethno-nationalist state in a new world order built on the sacred ground of blood and borders. "As the ideologist in Trump's inner circle," columnist Michael Gerson argues, "Bannon is a practitioner of Newt Gingrich's mystic arts. Take some partially valid insight at the crossroads of pop economics, pop history and pop psychology; declare it an inexorable world-historic force; and, by implication, take credit for being the only one who sees the inner workings of reality."[5] Bannon's "fourth turning" (did you Google it?), or the current moment in history, when the old order collapses and a new one is built on its ashes, foresees the end of Great Power America and the brutal birth of a zero-sum world of competing ethno-states.

"I think strong countries and strong nationalist movements in countries make strong neighbors," Bannon said at a 2014 Vatican conference, "and that is really the building blocks that built Western Europe and the United States."[6] These were the same building blocks that led to centuries of war, stopped only by the post-World War II economic integration brought about by the European Union, an integration Bannon openly wants to undo. The result: a system based on "spheres of influence," says distinguished diplomat Dan Fried, "admired by those who don't have to suffer the consequences." Accepting such a world would "mean our acquiescence when great powers, starting with China and Russia, dominated their neighbors through force and fear… A sphere of influence system would lead to cycles of rebellion and repression, and, if the past 1,000 years is any guide, lead to war between the great powers, because no power would be satisfied with its sphere. They never are."[7]

Bannon's Revenge Fantasy Goes Realsies

As journalist Jennifer Rubin argues, there's pretty much only one thing on Steve Bannon's mind, and it's a **"determination to destroy the liberal international order that has kept world war at bay and promoted global prosperity since the end of World War II."** He's spouted it over and over, he's given speeches about it, even made eyeball-searing, scare-the-pants-off-your-grandmother movies about it. "Bannon and Trump are living out a cultural revenge fantasy," she concludes, "[and] remain bonded to their base not because of ideology or agenda, but because they desire the downfall of coastal and urban elites (personified by the media), detest the ethnic and racial demographic trends that continue to make the country more diverse and hold fast to various myths and an exaggerated sense of victimhood (e.g. climate change is a hoax, minorities all live in violent and poverty-stricken cities, Christians are 'persecuted'). No wonder the Trump team finds a role model in the anti-Western, authoritarian Russian President Vladimir Putin, who runs a kleptocracy that impoverishes his people, whom he then tries to pacify with grandiose nationalistic ambitions."[8]

And on this side of the Pond, those grandiose nationalistic ambitions start with building…

Fortress America

… where Lady Liberty, instead of lighting the way for the world's huddled masses, demands you unlock your smartphone and hand over your passwords to even consider winning the privilege of stepping onto these shores. "Foreigners who want to visit the U.S., even for a short trip," political reporter Laura Meckler reports, "could be forced to disclose contacts on their mobile phones, social-media passwords and financial records, and to answer probing questions about their ideology." With extended interviews, and deep dives into everyone's online history, it's a process that could significantly stretch already-beleaguered diplomatic staff and cause far longer waits for even the most basic tourist visa.

What it will do is impoverish the access of ordinary Americans to foreign visitors and voices—and further alienate and distort Americans' image of the world and other cultures—while devastating the one weapon the United States has used to far greater effect than any other postwar nation: soft power. "There is no weapon or wall that is more powerful for American security," writes Garry Kasparov, "than America being envied, imitated, and admired around the world, as it was when I looked at it from afar from the Soviet Union. **Admired not for being perfect, but for having the exceptional courage to always try to be better.**"[9]

"We have to win. We have to start winning wars again."
                                        Donald Trump, the White House[10]

Those wars may have already begun and none of us would know. The administration has pledged not to publically release information on rising troop deployments to Syria and Iraq.[11] While in Yemen, a single "weeklong blitz" of bombing has eclipsed the total for any single year under Obama. And the escalation in Yemen—already a clusterfuck Saudi invasion marked by gross human rights violations on all sides and the mass killings of civilians—is only beginning.[12]

Not like he didn't warn us...

"Bomb the shit out of 'em...,"

... as Trump roared at a campaign rally in November 2015, describing his strategy to defeat ISIS, "I would just bomb those suckers, and that's right, I'd blow up the pipes, I'd blow up the refineries, **I'd blow up every single inch—there would be nothing left!"**[13]

If reports of sharply spiking civilian deaths in Iraq and Syria are accurate, then US rules of engagement have already dramatically changed and we may not be far from the indiscriminate slaughter of thousands, if not tens of thousands, of innocents. *Newsweek* **reports that as many as 1,500 civilians have been feared killed by Trump-authorized airstrikes in little more than the first two months of his administration**[14]—a staggering multifold increase over the last months of Obama's tenure, which itself was marked by rising airstrikes and civilian deaths in renewed offensives to push ISIS out of Mosul and other cities.

... or Count your Holy Wars

The targets here, all Muslim-majority nations, reflect a world seen through the dystopia-tinted shades of Steve Bannon, where a threatened Judeo-Christian West must destroy a rising and ungodly radical Islam to survive. "Rejected by most serious scholars of religion and shunned by Presidents George W. Bush and Barack Obama, this dark view of Islam has nonetheless flourished on the fringes of the American right since before the Sept. 11, 2001, terrorist attacks. With Mr. Trump's election, it has now moved to the center of American decision-making on security and law, alarming many Muslims."[15]

Bannon's never been shy to call a holy war just that. "**I believe you should take a very, very, very aggressive stance against radical Islam,**" he said at that 2014 Vatican conference. "If you look back at the long history of the Judeo-Christian West struggle against Islam, I believe that our forefathers kept their stance, and I think they did the right thing. I think they kept it out of the world, whether it was at Vienna, or Tours, or other places... It bequeathed to us the great institution that is the church of the West."[16]

And with God on your side, and God to defend, who counts the "collateral damage"?—or the lives of tens, or hundreds, of thousands of innocent Muslims and others across the Middle East. Historian David Kaiser was repeatedly pushed, in an interview for one of Bannon's documentaries, "to prompt him into saying that the US was on the brink of a third world war... [a war] *at least* as big as the Second World War."[17] And Bannon hasn't been shy about his own thoughts on the topic, saying in November 2015 that, "**We're clearly going into, I think, a major shooting war in the Middle East again.**"[18]

Donald Trump's repeated campaign promise to "rip up" the ground-breaking nuclear deal President Obama reached with Iran—"the most important arms control agreement in decades"[19]—is one possible path to Bannon's major shooting war; others include Vietnam-like escalations in Syria and Yemen, or a return of massive US ground forces to Iraq and Afghanistan, or any number of possibilities, including conflicts in Sudan, Somalia, Libya, and Egypt.

"We're going to war in the South China Sea, there's no doubt about that."

... Bannon assured his tinfoil-hat-sporting listeners in March 2016 on *Breitbart Radio*.[20] Apparently, China was listening, or certainly have been ever since Secretary of State Rex Tillerson warned at his confirmation hearing that "we're going to have to send China a clear signal that, first, the island-building stops and, second, your access to those islands also is not going to be allowed."[21] He was referring to disputed South China Sea islands China claims as its own, and on which it is building extensive military bases. The threat, if carried through, is tantamount to a declaration of war, senior Chinese military officials quickly cautioned, with the *People's Daily*, the official Communist Party outlet, writing, **"'A war within the president's term' or 'war breaking out tonight' are not just slogans, they are becoming a practical reality."**[22]

That (Way) Old Thucydides Trap

Harvard's Kennedy School professor and political scientist Graham Allison warns of the insanely unstable dynamic produced when a rising nation threatens the position of the dominant power, as Athens once did to Sparta. He calls it the "Thucydides Trap," adding that "[China's President] Xi and President Barack Obama even discussed the Thucydides Trap at their 2015 summit, but could not agree what to do to escape it." The odds aren't good.

"A major nation's rise has disrupted the position of a dominant state 16 times over the past 500 years. In 12 of those 16 cases, the outcome was war."

The paths to such a war, he adds, are multifold: any Trump administration move to recognize Taiwan's independence, which it has warned it might do, would surely spark one; as would a US invasion of North Korea to snuff out their nuclear program (which the Trump administration has all but promised if China refuses to pressure the North into falling into line); an escalation of the war of words over the South China Sea into a US blockade could easily spread; as could the quickly rising tension over Trump's claims that China is "raping" US businesses.[23]

Such a conflict, warns *The Independent*, after talking to several experts, "would be catastrophic, throwing the entire globe into turmoil… [and would] set off a global economic crisis and create a potential power vacuum inside defeated China 'the like of which we can't imagine.'" It even has a few (and hopefully overblown) genuine apocalypse Klaxons blaring, with Trevor McCrisken, associate professor of politics and international studies at the University of Warwick, arguing "that if war broke out [between the United States and China] 'we would be looking, I would imagine, at World War Three... I really do think that would be the end of life as we know it on Earth.'"[24]

But hey, if China doesn't work out, there's always Russia...

While Trump rage-tweets, a frustrated Vladimir Putin quietly plans, writes Garry Kasparov on the fizzling of a Russia-style "reset" of relations between the two nations. "The next step may come in the Balkans, in the Middle East, or closer to Russia, but it will come," warns the former Soviet dissident. **"Putin needs constant conflict to justify his hold on total power in Russia, and if he can't boast of a grand bargain with the new American President, he will need something else to distract the Russian people from their disintegrating homeland."**[25]

"If we have them, why can't we use them?"

If you are defending God, or Steve Bannon's righteous Judeo-Christian West against the evils of Islam, why not use every God-given weapon at your disposal? Trump's nuke woody goes back decades—with him even expressing a desire to personally negotiate nuclear policy with the Soviets.[26] In 1984, he told Lois Romano he could learn about missiles instantly: "It would take an hour-and-a-half to learn everything there is to learn about missiles... I think I know most of it anyway. You're talking about just getting updated on a situation... I'd do it in a second."[27]

The deal with the Soviets never happened, but Trump's obsession kept spinning in his head. "I've always thought about the issue of nuclear war; it's a very important element in my thought process," he said in 1990. "It's the ultimate, the ultimate catastrophe, the biggest problem this world has, and nobody's focusing on the nuts and bolts of it. It's a little like sickness. People don't believe they're going to get sick until they do. Nobody wants to talk about it. I believe the greatest of all stupidities is people's believing it will never happen, because everybody knows how destructive it will be, so nobody uses weapons. What bullshit."[28]

MSNBC's Joe Scarborough claimed that at a briefing on nuclear weapons in 2016, Donald Trump asked three times, "If we have them, why can't we use them?"—each time apparently unable to understand the nuance of the reasons why not.[29] The tale, hearsay from a briefing that happened months earlier, may or may not be true; but with Chris Matthews, when pressed, Trump refused again and again to disavow the first strike use of nuclear weapons, not only in the Middle East, but against Europe.[30]

"Well, just say it," Matthews pushed, asking Trump to promise never to use nuclear weapons against European allies.

To which Trump replied:

"I am not—I am not taking cards off the table."

X.
Revenge of the Basement Trolls

"The people are the only censors of their governors: and even their errors will tend to keep these to the true principles of their institution. To punish these errors too severely would be to suppress the only safeguard of the public liberty. The way to prevent these irregular interpositions of the people is to give them full information of their affairs thro' the channel of the public papers, & to contrive that those papers should penetrate the whole mass of the people. The basis of our governments being the opinion of the people, the very first object should be to keep that right; and were it left to me to decide whether we should have a government without newspapers or newspapers without a government, I should not hesitate a moment to prefer the latter."

Thomas Jefferson, Letter to Edward Carrington, 1787

"Fuck your feelings"

... or so "alt-right" transnational provocateur Milo Yiannopolous barked at a female questioner after a speech he gave at American University when asked if he was concerned whether his "controversial rhetoric 'invalidated' minority views."[1]

The bizarre amalgam that is the so-called "alt-right"—or as we used to call it, plain, unabashed white nationalism—the 4chan *hentai*-addicted basement trolls, the Ivy League-reject self-styled intellectual skinheads, the white male self-actualized professional victims, the hateful Twitterati endlessly retweeting Pepe the Frog memes each time someone coughs in the direction of one of their sainted heroes—is little more than the three-way hate-child of the self-immolating fantasies of what is called conservative "thought" these days, the seeming inability of the progressive left to offer little more than hand-wringing and the crawling fog of bureaucratic incrementalism, and a pop culture laid waste on the stone altar of soul-eating LULZ. Add to that a daily dose of fake news, right wing quackery and a paranoia-inducing (induced?) distrust of basic expertise and facts, and you have a growing segment of today's youth searching for certainty in the hard-rock walls of extremist thought.

What's new is always old...

It should be no surprise that it was a moment of casual misogyny by a member of the online community 4chan that sparked what became much of the modern alt-right—and thus vomited Milo Yiannopoulos and his hate-filled compadres into our collective laps. Writer and artist Dale Beran, who watched the rise of the movement from the inside, writes: "In 2014, a jilted lover claimed his ex-girlfriend had been unfaithful to him. He tried to prove to the internet that he was wronged in an embarrassing and incoherent blog post. The target of his post, his ex, happened to be a female game developer."[2]

#Gamergate: the Boy-Turd Nerds Go to War

Yiannopoulos first rose to prominence as ringmaster of the Gamergate orgy of not-so-virtual hate—an all-out onslaught on what 4chan members called SJWs—Social Justice Warriors—who were for the most part female game developers arguing for a more inclusive and less violently misogynistic gaming experience. Already a self-avowed woman hater—"[Yiannopoulos] argues that men no longer need be interested in women, that they can and should walk away from the female sex *en masse*"—he offered a rallying cry for the loser in the basement, the oft-humiliated troll who knew his life was gurgling in circles around the bottom of the toilet drain.[3]

In much of the "alt-right" world, porn, masturbation, sex dolls, prostitutes or total abstinence become morally and functionally superior to actual live, breathing (and yes, talking) women in a

mythical United States of Bro-dom. Many, including Yiannopoulos, openly celebrate a future of sex bots when the women, in their puerile, reality-starved imaginations, will become obsolete—it'll be swinging dicks from San Fran to DC while walkin' not-so-much-talkin' AI Fleshlights satisfy those still desperately clinging to their inner vagina monologues.

"Peaceful ethnic cleansing"

In the days after Donald Trump's election victory, standard-bearers of the newly invigorated "alt-right" and white nationalist movements descended on DC in veritable Panzer squadrons, including organizing the DeploraBall to celebrate inauguration night itself.[4] Wanting to jettison their more Nazi-fied elements, they were hoping to rebrand themselves as straight-up nationalists—not so easy when one of their leaders, Richard Spencer led attendees in a rousing, *zeig heil*-ing chorus of "Hail Trump! Hail Trump! Hail Trump!" in the cavernous bowels of the Ronald Reagan building.[5]

He was already the standard-bearer of the "alt-right"—even before he got his face clocked by an anonymous attacker on live TV—in fact, he coined the term and appeared "on NPR and CNN to defend what he calls 'European identitarianism,' and what others call, with less varnish, racism. **He sports the alt-right's signature shaved-side haircut—the 'fashy,' as in fascist—and leads the benignly named National Policy Institute, a think tank with an office in Arlington, Virginia, to push his vision for [in Spencer's own phrase] 'peaceful ethnic cleansing.'"[6]**

But Spencer, much like Milo and the resurfacing of his snarky advocacy of pedophilia as a healthy child-rearing practice (*don't say it if you don't want people to hear it, Milo!*), found that Hitler-boy love, much like man-boy love, was a line most in the far right didn't want to cross— at least not openly, preferring to distance themselves from the term "white nationalism"—Spencer's fig leaf nomenclature for a midcentury beer stein frothing with good ol' National Socialism.

"Nationalism," "populist nationalism," "white nationalism"—call it what you will, in the end someone gets hung from a tree, someone else gets rounded up, put in a camp and (if they're lucky) deported for no reason other than the color of their skin, while steroid-pumping jackasses with the emotional IQ of dried yeast flounce merrily about in pointy white hoods or ICE flak jackets, inadvertently posing, when they're not bare-knuckling a so-called "illegal" to the ground, for Tom of Finland reproductions.

"Children of the Sun"

… a phrase Spencer proudly spouted, describing himself and his oh-so-white followers, during his thunderous Nazi salute speech in the Ronald Reagan building—one which drew directly on the roots of modern fascism. Coined by Julius Evola, one of the wacko mystic soothsayers of Italian fascism, it described his "vision of a bourgeoisie smashing new order that he called the Solar Civilization."[7]

It's a vision Spencer has obviously embraced—as he has done with much else of Evolaspeak. "America was until this past generation a white country designed for ourselves and our posterity," Spencer said, echoing decades of extreme nativist thought. "It is our creation, it is our inheritance, and it belongs to us."[8] Citing what sounds like a villainous cult out of peak-1970s *Doctor Who*, the "Children of the Sun," he spoke to the heart of Evola's idea of the supernatural superiority of Western manhood. Evola's mystical beliefs led him to a total rejection of all things modern and decadent in favor of an uber-man, able to bend reality to his will. Humanism, the Renaissance, the Protestant Reformation, the French Revolution—all disasters for humanity in Evola's eyes, stripping us of the transcendent and stranding us in the muck of daily life.[9]

"Changing the system, Evola argued, was 'not a question of contesting and polemicizing, but *of blowing everything up.*'"[10]

Ring any bells?

It's not only fashy-sporting Spencer and the boy-turds of 4chan who found in Evola and others like him the mythic Wagnerian echoes of a lost island of little white boys to which they yearn to return.

It's also Harley-riding bad boy Steve Bannon who directly referenced Evola's thought in his talk to the Vatican—as sharp a dog whistle as could be to the intellectual (-ly challenged) leaders of the nutjob wing of the American fascist movement.[11]

XI.
Wagner on the Turntable

"Shall we expect some transatlantic military giant to step the ocean and crush us at a blow? Never! All the armies of Europe, Asia, and Africa combined, with all the treasure of the earth (our own excepted) in their military chest, with a Bonaparte for a commander, could not by force take a drink from the Ohio or make a track on the Blue Ridge in a trial of a thousand years. At what point then is the approach of danger to be expected? I answer. If it ever reach us it must spring up amongst us; it cannot come from abroad. If destruction be our lot we must ourselves be its author and finisher. As a nation of freemen we must live through all time or die by suicide."

Abraham Lincoln, Lyceum Address, 1838

Heads Up, Sheeple, Alt-Right's in da House

Stephen Miller, the thirty-one-year-old balding, gaunt-faced, permanently scowling, grim little white nationalist at the heart of Donald Trump's administration—another amorphous adviser wandering bleakly through the largely empty halls of the West Wing searching for the light switch—was early on "caught" throwing what looked exactly like a White Power symbol: one hand forming a W, the other a P. The photo wasn't a random snapshot either, with his hands accidentally and awkwardly raised, caught in midmotion, but an official White House image released to the press, and personally approved by Miller himself.[1]

But hey, perhaps he was having a bad day—looked for love in the wrong place—*who hasn't?*— thinking a few White Power homies in the crowd might show some?

Uhh...

"I can't be your friend...

... any more because you are Latino," said the very very long bad-day Miller, then age fourteen—and recently politicized by *Guns & Ammo* magazine—to his former best bud and fellow Trekkie, Jason Islas. Miller had vanished that summer, not bothering to return Islas's phone calls, until fall rolled round when he finally called and told him to go fuck himself.

"Islas recalled that Miller mentioned other reasons," writes Fernando Peinado, "which he considered 'childish.' But that was his first sign of the change Miller would undergo when he was fourteen years old: a political radicalization that defines his life even now as a senior White House adviser with direct access to President Donald Trump."[2]

"He had a lot of grudges. He didn't go out of his way to go to dances or to have girlfriends," another fellow student recalled. **"I don't remember ever seeing him smile."**[3]

Natalie Flores was blistering in her evaluation of the coauthor of Trump's apocalyptic inauguration speech, claiming, **"he displayed 'an intense hatred toward people of color, especially toward Latinos.'** She and other students... recalled that Miller became angry whenever he heard students speaking Spanish in the hallways."[4]

Spit-ball teen rebellion at all things multiculti in Birkenstock-nirvana Santa Monica, where Miller grew up, shouldn't be surprising in a socially awkward nerd. He's said as much : "When we think of non-conformity, we tend to imagine kids in the '60s rebelling against 'the system.'" Conjure the air-quotes yourself. "This was my system. My establishment was a dogmatic educational system that often uniformly expressed a single point of view."[5]

That he subsequently chose to sharpen and deepen his ethno-virulence is much more telling, becoming an aide to everyone's favorite right wing furies Michelle Bachmann and Jeff Sessions. In the White House, he's become "the epicenter of some of the administration's most provocative moves, from pushing hard for the construction of a wall along the border with Mexico to threatening decades-long trade deals at the heart of Republican economic orthodoxy, to rolling out Mr. Trump's travel ban on seven largely Muslim nations, whose bungled introduction he oversaw."[6]

In the soft-shouldered, weed-soaked political bonhomie of Southern California—where blacktop, sand, sea and sky heat-merge into a bland continuity—he learned that if you wanted to find an edge, you had to go for the extremes.

Or who knows, maybe he thought he'd look better in a pointy white hood?

Guest Alt-Euro DJ Gorka Spins Some Magyar Hate

When Sebastian Gorka stepped out into the fawning crowds on inauguration night, he had dumped his tux and wore instead "the uniform and medal of *Vitézi Rend*—the *bocskai*—a Hungarian order of merit closely associated with Nazi Germany."[7]

One top Hungarian academic, András Biro-Nagy of Budapest's Corvinus University, Allegra Kirkland reports, where Gorka also studied, says "the *bocskai* he wore was popular during [Nazi-allied] Horthy's rule and today is often worn by members of the 'right-wing' on special occasions." There's little doubting what wearing the medal means today. "The medal is a clear sign," Biro-Nagy said, "that he sympathizes with the Horthy era."[8]

One more dim bulb from the cabinet of 25-watt spares that is *Breitbart News*, Gorka's assumed yet another vaporous adviser role in Trump's foggy brain trust. Omid Safi, director of Islamic Studies at Duke University, didn't pull his punches in his assessment, labeling

Gorka's book, *New York Times* bestseller *Defeating Jihad: The Winnable War*, "propaganda." And saying, **"He opines on everything from the Koran to Mohamad to jihad to Islamic history to contemporary politics but does so in a way that is inaccurate, sloppy, superficial, bigoted and ideological,"[9]**

In addition to helping scrawl in crayon Trump Inc's *shut 'em all out and slam the doors* policy toward Islam and the Middle East, Gorka has been one of its more efficient German shepherds in attacking the press, snarling at any news organization that so much as rolls its eyes at the president and barking that they're "fake news"—going so far as to say *any* attacks on the president are false and **"that the administration will continue using the term 'fake news' until the media understands that their 'monumental desire' to attack the President is wrong."[10]**

Michael Anton Storms the Cockpit

Donning the good ol' boy blue collar hero moniker Publius Decius Mus, a Roman consul who in 340 BC sacrificed himself at the Battle of Vesuvius by violently charging the enemy in a blood-curdling display of unrestrained violence and extraordinary gore, Michael Anton, another nebulous adviser to the president, argued in his essay "The Flight 93 Election" that the 2016 election was THE *do or die moment* for American conservatism and the American republic. Either way, the odds weren't good: **"a Hillary Clinton presidency is Russian Roulette with a semi-auto. With Trump, at least you can spin the cylinder and take your chances."[11]**

A time for all good conservatives, he sputtered, like passengers on the ill-fated American Airlines Flight 93 on September 11, 2001, to charge the cockpit and go for broke—damn the consequences. The consequences in that case being collective death.[12]

An out and out America Firster—he was the 260-pound linebacker defending Trump's co-opting of the openly racist term, once used by

Klan members and vocal American anti-Semites—he argued in an earlier essay, excerpted at where else but *Breitbart*, for a stridently nationalist Christian vision of America as a land *conquered by* Europeans and *solely for* Europeans, openly scorning the nation's immigrant legacy.

"[One] source of Trump's appeal is his willingness—eagerness—gleefulness!—to mock the ridiculous lies we've been incessantly force-fed for the past 15 years (at least) and tell the truth. **'Diversity' is not 'our strength'; it's a source of weakness, tension and disunion. America is not a 'nation of immigrants'; we are originally a nation of settlers, who later chose to admit immigrants,** and later still not to, and who may justly open or close our doors solely at our own discretion, without deference to forced pieties. Immigration today is not 'good for the economy'; it undercuts American wages, costs Americans jobs, and reduces Americans' standard of living. Islam is not a 'religion of peace'; it's a militant faith that exalts conversion by the sword and inspires thousands to acts of terror—and millions more to support and sympathize with terror."[13]

Inventing the straw-man enemy of a monolithic "Islam" bent on the imposition of universal "Sharia Law" and the destruction of the West, he went on to write, **"Islam and the modern West are incompatible... Only an insane society, or one desperate to prove its fidelity to some chimerical 'virtue,' would have increased Muslim immigration after the September 11th attacks. Yet that is exactly what the United States did.** Trump has, for the first time, finally forced the questions: Why? And can we stop now?"[14]

But Hey, Ain't No One Spinning Wagner for Realsies

Let's take Trump and his administration at their word: **they're not racists, they're plain old-fashioned *nationalists*.** But it's a particular kind of nationalism, closer to tribalism—in this case unabashed and unapologetic **white tribalism.**

Who knows what Donald Trump truly thinks of African Americans, Muslims, Jews, Middle Easterners, Indians, Mexicans, Whatever-ans? We do know what he thinks of "white" people—

… because each time a "white" person is attacked somewhere in the known universe in what he perceives as hate or terror-related, he takes to Twitter to bellow his condemnation, often in all-caps. This tells us a great deal—the nation in "nationalism" that he sees reflects himself: a successful white male—the rest of us just live here and either need to get along or get out.

How do we know? Because the world he sees is one where a "white" cop slightly injured in Paris is worth far more indignation than six Muslims brutally murdered in Quebec or an Indian American killed in Kansas.

When you're president, and the people you care about, the people you reward, the people you choose to protect, are your tribe and *only* your tribe, then it no longer matters whether you're a racist or not—your actions do all the talking…

… because you're ignoring, devaluing, and endangering the very real lives of African, Muslim, Jewish, Sikh, Hindu, Latino, Chinese, Japanese, Gay, Lesbian, Bisexual, Trans—and basically every American who isn't "white" and "straight"—or the rest of the actual living, breathing wildly eclectic *nation*.

XII.
Donald Does Berlin

"The jaws of power are always open to devour, and her arm is always stretched out, if possible, to destroy the freedom of thinking, speaking, and writing."

John Adams, A Dissertation on the Canon and Feudal Law, 1765

"Look at Putin—what he's doing with Russia— I mean this guy has done—whether you like him or don't like him..."

Donald Trump, CNN[1]

... yeah, Donald... sometimes, it no longer matters what comes out of his mouth: He loves Putin, he hates the guy, he trusts him more than Obama, he's the only guy able to be tough on him. So it goes, as Kurt Vonnegut said, who perhaps better than anyone dissected the self-serving hypocrisies of rich and vanity-addled men who send boys off to die in pointless wars. But while over the last twenty years Donald Trump has been practicing his presidential acceptance speech in front of a vulgarian's vulgarian gold-rimmed mirror, Vladimir Putin and others have been transforming the way the world actually runs.

The Rise of "Illiberal Democracy"

It's a term coined by political commentator Fareed Zakaria in 1997 and describes a soft departure from political systems governed "not only by free and fair elections, but also by the rule of law, a separation of powers, and the protection of basic liberties of speech, assembly, religion, and property." In the illiberal democracy, the cover of so-called "free" elections serve to mask that some, or many, of those protections have either seriously eroded or been lost altogether. "The greatest danger that illiberal democracy poses—other than to its own people—is that it will discredit liberal democracy itself, casting a shadow on democratic governance."[2]

Twenty years on and many of the predictions Zakaria made are coming true. "The resurgence of authoritarian attitudes and practices that first manifested itself in young democracies, such as Russia, Thailand and the Philippines," writes journalist Gideon Rachman, "has spread into western politics. Poland and Hungary have governments with authoritarian tendencies. The most dramatic development is the election of a US president who regards the free press as 'the enemy' and has little respect for an independent judiciary."[3]

Citing much-discussed research by Roberto Foa and Yascha Mounk, Rachman highlights a startling rise of anti-democratic sentiments across the West. "One of their more eye-catching points is that one-in-six Americans now think that it would be a good idea for the 'army to rule'—up from one in 16 in 1995. And while more than 70 per cent of Americans born in the 1930s think it 'essential' to live in a democracy, only 30 per cent of those born in the 1980s agree."[4]

But Really—in Europe?

In Poland for sure, where "the Law and Justice party has undermined and disempowered the constitutional court," writes journalist Anne Applebaum, "politicized the civil service, and turned public media into a crude party propaganda organ. The defense minister wants to create a 'territorial army' that would be directly responsible to him and not part of the chain of command." She calls it out for what it is, a "glaring example of illiberal democracy… where a legitimately elected government is breaking the constitution, both in letter and in spirit."[5] In a 2014 speech, Hungarian Prime Minister Viktor Orban pledged to end liberal democracy. "I don't think that our European Union membership precludes us from building an illiberal new state based on national foundations," Orban said, citing Russia, Turkey and China as models of "successful" so-called democracies.[6] The watchdog group Freedom House reported that as of 2017 both nations had undergone a "spectacular breakdown in democracy."[7]

The rising strength of illiberal movements in France, the Netherlands, Italy, Greece and the United Kingdom, while not yet close to the degradation of political life in Poland and Hungary, pose serious risks for Europe's democratic future. And Turkey, as Tezcan Gumus writes, "is about to use democracy to end their democracy."[8] A recently concluded referendum now threatens to introduce one-person autocratic rule under President (for life?) Recip Tayyip Erdogan. Yay referendums!

European Disunion

Donald Trump's trash-talking NATO—calling it "obsolete"[9]—and the EU—predicting more countries would be leaving the bloc after the UK referendum to cut ties[10]—are like pulling up an oil tanker and letting it pour onto the illiberal fires spreading across the continent. He'd grudgingly back-pedal the above comments, told to the *Sunday Times* and Germany's *Bild* weeks before taking office, but the damage was already done. It didn't help that his touted pick for EU ambassador, Ted Malloch, told the BBC that the euro would be dead within eighteen months. And asked whether the United States would soon finalize a trade deal with the EU, Malloch responded, "I personally am not certain that there will be a European Union with which to have such negotiations."[11]

Dovetailing with Vladimir Putin's own years-long ambition to take a hammer to the bloc, Trump's obsession with European disintegration—and the genuine fear that he might actually work to foster that goal—has caused no end of panic in European capitals, forcing German Chancellor Angela Merkel to say, "I think we Europeans have our fate in our own hands,"[12] an extraordinary admission from a leader who had one of the closest relationships with President Obama. While EU President Jean-Claude Juncker, has (presumably jokingly) threatened to support secessionist movements in Ohio and Texas if Trump doesn't tone down his anti-EU language.[13]

There are plenty of avenues open if Trump chooses to follow through: from supporting extremist, anti-EU candidates to offering sweetheart trade deals to nations that choose to go it alone. But it's a path that would seriously destabilize the region, writes Harold James, "as old national rivalries are unleashed again. In the past, Americans saw Europe as a pole of stability in an uncertain world. **The new vision wants European instability, political as well as economic.** The end result is that Europe would be more fractious—indeed, more like Donald Trump's America."[14]

A Requiem for Small-D Democracy?

It turns out that *small-d* democracy is a far more fragile creature than many of us believed, and one, when it weakens or dies, creates the potential for genuine chaos. "What sustains democracy is not simply legal safeguards and rules," writes Fareed Zakaria in a reappraisal of his old essay, "but norms and practices—*democratic behavior*. This culture of liberal democracy is waning in the United States today… [and] we are now getting to see what American democracy looks like without any real buffers in the way of sheer populism and demagoguery. The parties have collapsed, Congress has caved, professional groups are largely toothless, the media have been rendered irrelevant. What we are left with today is an open, meritocratic, competitive society in which everyone is an entrepreneur, from a congressman to an accountant, always hustling for personal advantage. But who and what remain to nourish and preserve the common good, civic life and liberal democracy?"[15]

Or as staunchly conservative Senator John McCain said in an April 2017 interview[16]:

"I am more worried about this country than I've been in my entire lifetime."

XIII.
Billionaires Gotta Billionaire

"A power to dispose of estates for ever is manifestly absurd. The earth and the fulness of it belongs to every generation, and the preceding one can have no right to bind it up from posterity. Such extension of property is quite unnatural."

Adam Smith, Lectures on Jurisprudence, 1763

The Billionaire (Mostly) Boys Club...

… who want to take an ax to the US government…

… to give huge tax breaks…

… to billionaires like themselves…

.., otherwise known as Trump's cabinet… where a mere four of them combined—Betsy DeVos, Wilbur Ross, Linda McMahon and Rex Tillerson—**own the accumulated wealth of more than one third of all Americans.**[1] This doesn't even include The Donald's supposed wealth, or the other billionaires and sad-sack millionaires in Trump's Team of Silver Spooners. Nor does it include the small-fry, where the combined wealth of twenty-seven White House officials equals at least $2.3 billion.[2]

But at least *they're* qualified…?

… though not to *do* their jobs, but *undo* them.

Steve Bannon admitted as much in a speech at the triumphant CPAC 2017—the annual Christian conservative Hajj, where instead of stoning a pillar representing the devil, attendees hurl verbal insults at the devil of "big—or any—government" and "the secular state"—indeed, if they'd bother to read it, most would think Margaret Atwood's *The Handmaid's Tale* is more utopian guidebook than dystopian fantasy. This year they were pranked into waving Russian flags with Trump's name emblazoned on them while waiting for the president to address the crowd.[3] While the flags were snatched away before the president spoke, their loony-tunes devotion to all things theocratic and un-(*big-D*)-Democratic remained.

Trump's speech was overshadowed by his deputy's, Steve Bannon, who decided to shed his Cloak of Invisibility back at the National Security Council and replace it with what Richard Wolffe described as "his mask of death." The *real* threat to the nation, he yelled, was a critical media he'd already dubbed "the opposition party," calling them "the corporatist, globalist media that are adamantly opposed to the economic nationalist agenda that Donald Trump has."[4]

And why? Because they're one of the major roadblocks to the heart of the Bannon/Trump agenda:

"The Deconstruction of the Administrative State"

Bannon was unapologetic about Trump's newly forming cabinet, and didn't mince words about why so many were chosen who either had no experience in their assigned roles, or had spent careers actively opposing and undermining the offices they were now about to hold.

"If you look at these cabinet appointees," he said, "they were selected for a reason and that is the deconstruction. The way the progressive left runs, is if they can't get it passed, they're just going to put in some sort of regulation in an agency. That's all going to be deconstructed and I think that that's why this regulatory thing is so important."[5]

This "regulatory thing," explains Max Fisher, "portrays the problem as flowing from something deeper: a shadowy 'administrative state' engineered by the left to advance its agenda. **The state, in this view, is not an instrument of the American electorate, nor even a hurdle to be overcome as mainline conservatives often see it, but rather an adversary innately hostile to the people.**"[6]

Who needs details when you have a job to do?

The job—Bannon's so-called "deconstruction of the administrative state"—is a radical reshaping of all aspects of US government, how it works, who it's for, what it does and doesn't do, its most basic duties and relationship to the citizenry—oops, now we're "customers," according to Jared Kushner, Trump's son-in-law who was tapped to lead the new "White House Office of American Innovation"—tasked with finding *profit-driven* solutions to so-called government waste or obsolescence.

"Our hope is that we can achieve successes and efficiencies for our customers, who are the citizens."[7]

"Customers" of the only game in town, so if you think cable company customer service blows chunks on a good day, imagine the forest that phone tree will lead you through and how long you'll be listening to Muzak purchased by the last bureaucrat with a paycheck when it's ringing in the deserted, Ryan budget-starved offices of the new federal government-*ultralite edition*. Can you hear me echo now?

Trump's first budget proposal, released in March, envisions massive and crippling across-the-board cuts to almost all agencies, with some being gutted or eliminated entirely. "The warning to Americans from the government is clear: your national defense will be well-funded and your security will be a priority," writes politics reporter Gregory Krieg, "but for benefits beyond the most basic services, don't count on me...

"… It's a kind of break-up note to taxpayers. Uncle Sam can still be your friend, sure, but that's it. Nothing more."[8]

Anyhoo, no worries because it *is guaranteed*…

Compassionate… to Taxpayers

… argues White House budget chief and a tax cutter's tax cutter…

Mick Mulvaney

"Meals on Wheels sounds great," Mulvaney said during a White House news briefing, and added, "we're not going to spend on programs that cannot show that they actually deliver the promises that we've made to people." The budget blueprint he presented calls for radical cuts to domestic programs in exchange for massively increased military spending, and described it as:

"One of the most compassionate things we can do."

The compassion, Mulvaney promised, was reserved for the taxpayer, arguing all the programs cut were ineffective. "You're only focusing on half of the equation, right?" he continued, "You're focusing on recipients of the money. We're trying to focus on both the recipients of the money and the folks who give us the money in the first place. And I think it's fairly compassionate to go to them and say, 'Look, we're not going to ask you for your hard-earned money anymore … unless we can guarantee to you that that money is actually going to be used in a proper function.' And I think that is about as compassionate as you can get."[9]

XIV.
Goodbye, America?

"Sometimes it is said that man cannot be trusted with the government of himself. Can he, then, be trusted with the government of others?"

Thomas Jefferson, Inaugural Address, 1801

Drag US to Hell

Donald Trump's rogues' gallery of a cabinet, house wreckers mostly installed to bring the walls tumbling down around them, are as much nightmares from the fever dream of Bannon's vow to gut the administrative state as they are from Trump's own American carnage vision of the only path to genuinely making America great again.

As he told *Fox & Friends* in 2014, the road to renewal starts with not-so-creative-destruction[1]:

"When the economy crashes, when the country goes to *total* hell and everything is a disaster. Then you'll have a,"—*chuckling*—"you know, you'll have riots to go back to where we used to be when we were great."

It's hard to imagine a president who wants the economy to crash, riots to break out, social order to collapse—and his Trumpocalypse to MAGA vision probably tells us more about what age his impoverished, Hollywood-disaster-flick-fueled imagination stalled at—preteen, at a guess—than actual intentions.

But those actual intentions... let's look at a few of them more closely.

Sticking It to You and Me

... by outright killing, or at the very least, neutering, the power of the Consumer Financial Protection Bureau has long been an aim of Republicans, and at least two bills moving through Congress would either eliminate the agency, or leave as little more than a "toy poodle," as Senator Sherrod Brown termed it. The legislation would "greatly shrink the enforcement tools at the consumer watchdog's disposal, blocking it from being able to go after businesses engaged in deceptive practices and restricting its oversight of big publicly traded companies." In its few short years in existence, the agency has saved 27 million Americans as much as $12 billion.[2]

Privatizing Infrastructure

... so US and foreign corporations charge us for the privilege of driving on our own roads or across our own bridges, as Secretary of Transportation Elaine Chao face-planted as she tripped over her own words and admitted to Fox News's Sean Hannity:

"So, basically, we allow foreign inv—uh, we allow different kinds of money, private sector money *to come into* the United States—*I'm not saying foreign*—to come and fund, let's say a bridge or a road or it can be any kind of infrastructure."

Hannity called it a "win-win" where corporations "get their invest-ment back by having a toll on that road and that's where the taxpayers don't pay a penny, they make a profit."[3] On Trump's pay-to-play de-regulation expressway, the rest of us will be stuck in the pay-as-you-go lanes.

"The Most Dangerous Bill You've Never Heard Of..."

... argues Carl Pope, describing the nightmare REINS Act. Already passed by the House and waiting for Senate approval, the legislation "requires that any future major regulation adopted by an Executive Agency—say a new toxic chemical standard required by the recent-ly enacted Chemical Safety Act, or a new consumer protection rule about some innovative but untested kind of food additive—must be approved by a specific resolution in each House of Congress within 70 days to take effect." The implications are staggering—and would effectively neuter most health and safety bills, even those currently on the books. Even if Congress *wanted*—and that's a big if—to approve a specific rule change, it would be near impossible in the given time frame and the Congressional workload. In the past, the Senate has refused to pass it—but 2017 is like no year before and no word yet either way.[4]

Erasing Science

... literally. Arctic researcher Victoria Herrmann explains that word spread quickly in the science community after Trump's win to begin downloading and backing up the truly massive amount of basic scien-tific data held in US government databases and servers, out of fear the new administration would delete it. The researchers weren't wrong, and on January 21, the day after the inauguration, "the distress flare of lost data came as a surge of defunct links." That was barely the beginning. "Since January," she writes, "the surge has transformed into a slow, incessant march of deleting datasets, webpages and pol-icies about the Arctic. I now come to expect a weekly email request to replace invalid citations, hoping that someone had the foresight to download statistics about Arctic permafrost thaw or renewable energy in advance of the purge."[5] Other administration officials have chosen to simply discredit the idea of science altogether. One unnamed climate spokesperson, when questioned by reporters, claimed to have never heard of supposed studies linking rising sea levels with economic damage, asking the reporters to please forward the studies.[6]

Hello Detroit... the New Everytown

... because cuts to the EPA require that to ensure even basic maintenance "to administer waste treatment and drinking water" programs the rest of the budget needs to be cut by a staggering 43 percent. "The Trump administration says the EPA cuts reflect a philosophy of limiting federal government and devolving authority to the states, localities and, in some cases, corporations." Research would be drastically slashed or eliminated for programs on climate change, water quality, and chemical safety—and even research for "safe and sustainable water resources." Cut along with these would be programs that "study known environmental hazards including lead, poor indoor air quality, and radiation... [and] that help protect Americans from cancer."[7]

And oh yes...

The Golden Ring...

... that much-fabled GOP prize, one that's been giving the GOP wet dreams for years and that would bring in billions upon billions of dollars for their already ludicrously rich-beyond-imagination backers while stripping ordinary Americans of one of their last, fig leaf protections against sickness, poverty and old age: strangling Obamacare, drowning Medicaid, selling Medicare and Social Security off to the highest bidder, and repealing the already ludicrously low estate tax, thus enthroning a permanent class of the disgustingly ultra ultra rich for generations to come. With shoddily rushed passage of the Tax Cuts and Jobs Act of 2017—a one way transfer of the wealth of working and middle class Americans to a sliver of the nation's richest one percent and widely derided as the "big heist"—and its resultant ballooning deficits, Paul Ryan is already arguing that entitlement programs must be next on the GOP's butcher block in coming months.[8]

Either way, this is only...

The Opening Salvo...

... and many of these programs bring money and jobs to congressional Republicans in deep Red State America, and so will be defended vigorously in both the House and Senate. But as Chris Mooney writes,

"Even deeper cuts are expected to be sought for 2018."[9]

So if it's not gone this go-round, wait for next year... because one way or another, that god-awful Neanderthal unibrow of Trump, Bannon, and Ryan aren't going to stop until they've sliced the last tendon from their libertarian walking skeleton of a not-so-much government.

But in an age of absolute "personal responsibility," the one function government will want to support is a constitutionally mandated public education, right—because without a strong start, how can anyone hope to navigate the sand traps of dog-eat-dog capitalism or learn when to stick in the proverbial knife before your opponent guts you.

Believe that, I've got some sure-fire Greek bank stocks to sell you, because...

"I love the poorly educated."

... as Donald Trump said at a Las Vegas campaign rally,[10]

or, Betsy DeVos, Case Study in Crapitude

Not only is Betsy DeVos a billionaire in her own right, she is the daughter of a billionaire, married to another billionaire, Dick DeVos Jr., who himself just happens to be the son of a *multi*billionaire.[11]

With a Plainspoken (Christian) Mission...

... to "advance God's kingdom" with taxpayer funds. "Our desire is to confront the culture in ways that will continue to advance God's kingdom," she said in 2001 at The Gathering, a meeting of hard-right Christian philanthropists. Her husband, sitting next to her, echoed her sentiments: "The church—which ought to be in *our view* far more central to the life of the community—has been displaced by the public school as the center for activity, the center for what goes on in the community... It is certainly *our hope* that churches would continue, no matter what the environment—whether it's **government funding some day through tax credits, or vouchers**, or some other mechanism...—that more and more churches will get more and more active and engaged in education."[12]

Or plainly put:

Dismantle public education as we know it by systematically starving it of dollars, that go instead to any variety of academically questionable for-profit schools or religious institutions, lining the pockets of corporations and/or replacing a plural, diverse secular education with the narrow constraints of religious indoctrination.

It's not the money... oh wait, it *is* the money...

When quizzed by Senator Bernie Sanders about her family's political donations, Betsy DeVos conceded that "maybe" they had contributed around $**200 million** to the Republican Party over the years.[13]

"My family is the largest single contributor of soft money to the national Republican party," DeVos baosted in a 1997 *Roll Call* op-ed. "I have decided, however, to stop taking offense at the suggestion that we are buying influence. *Now, I simply concede the point.* **We expect to foster a conservative governing philosophy consisting of limited government and respect for traditional American virtues. We expect a return on our investment**; we expect a good and honest government. Furthermore, we expect the Republican party to use the money to promote these policies, and yes, to win elections."[14]

So what's it all going to look like—toll roads, for profit schools, unfettered corporations, deregulated banks, government by tax voucher… and on and on. Say hello to…

Pay-As-U-Go America

… or the "sharing economy" goes nuclear…

… a roots-up reimagining of government—where instead of citizens banding together as a nation, we fend for ourselves, customers at best who only get served if we ante up the bucks, and even then often in the most basic ways—Ayn Rand's vision made walking zombie flesh. Imagine having to figure out if your water is clean enough to drink or if your air is safe to breathe or if a particular drug is helpful or not or if it might kill you or not knowing whether food is safe to eat—a free-for-all libertarian vision where the gloves are off for corporations to do whatever they want to us in the name of profit—because *hey, it should be up to us* to protect ourselves and our families. It might still be illegal to poison water or manufacture kill-you cars, but don't count on anyone being around to prosecute the villains. And if you want a government job with a pension, join the military, because defense will be one of the last sure-fire life gigs going in a country of competing, race-for-the-bottom-*stans*—Californiastan vs. Kentuckystan vs. Michiganstan—not states in a union.

In the end, kleptocrats gotta kleptocrat—*"rule by thieves, literally"*— and the final joke of the Trump presidency might be that this has all been one not-so-thinly-veiled initiation of a single man and his family into the transnational kleptocrat club—alongside the likes of Vladimir

Putin of Russia, Recep Tayyip Erdoğan of Turkey, Xi Jinping of China, and the Hindutva-spouting sycophants circling Narendra Modi in India—and with every freedom, economic opportunity, and basic belief in our fellow Americans he strips from us, he earns one more golden lapel pin, and a few more billions stashed in secret overseas accounts—all so that finally, the kid from Queens can play with the world's big boy bullies.

Afterword

How Democracy Dies, Not with a Bang, but with a Whimper?

"Love your country, but never trust its government."

Robert A. Heinlein[1]

The Age of Spectacle

Our worst fears seldom come true, and in politics, compromise and a shoddy, jerry-built halfway house between kicking the can down the road and making the best of a bad situation is usually what gets made. All things being equal, Donald Trump, like Richard Nixon before him, will fade into the rearview mirror of American corruption and criminality—and while for a time he may look bigger than he actually is, more heroic to some, more horrific to the rest of us, he'll likely shrivel in memory into the small-brained man-child he is, someone who tormented a nation with one truly outsized tantrum.

But all things are not always equal, and these are far from ordinary times.

In the past few months, while Donald Trump face-planted on his signature campaign promise to kill Obamacare, he's carried out an extra-legislative campaign to gut it and watch it bleed out to a slow death.[2] The newly minted Republican tax cut proposal promises, in the words of friend-to-every-billionaire *Fortune* magazine, to "be the biggest wealth grab in modern history."[3] John Kelly, the steady-hand chief of staff brought in to bring order to chaos in Trump's snake-pit inner sanctum, has outed himself a proud historical revisionist, peddling widely debunked ideas about the Civil War and slavery while showing his love for slave holder and perennial American loser Robert E. Lee.[4] All the while, Trump can't help reverting to his fantasy wrestling bravado as his retweet of an image showing a train slamming—or let's just say it, pounding, crushing, pulverizing—a CNN reporter only days after a car driven by an open white supremacist similarly slammed into a group of anti-fascist protestors in Charlottesville, Virginia, killing one.[5]

As the WrestleMania presidency normalizes, as day by day the unthinkable only a year ago becomes our new lived experience, as we watch a president relate to us, his fellow citizens, as little more than spectators in a reality television drama or screaming in an all-caps Twitter rage "DO SOMETHING!" and as the lockstep right-wing media machine, endlessly echoed by legions of paid trolls, Russian or otherwise, along with a fawning, intellectually defeated GOP, supplant basic common sense with the billionaire-friendly lies of tax-cut-or-die suicide bombers, we are left, wherever on the political spectrum, on the sidelines, watching as the fabric of modern American democracy frays to the point of tearing itself apart.

American essayist Adam Gopnik rightly warned in 2016, as Trump's popularity was rising, that if he won, "there is a decent chance that the American experiment would be over. This is not a hyperbolic prediction; it is not a hysterical prediction; it is simply a candid reading of what history tells us happens in countries with leaders like Trump. Countries don't really recover from being taken over by unstable authoritarian nationalists of any political bent, left or right—not by Peróns or Castros or Putins or Francos or Lenins or fill in the blanks. The nation may survive, but the wound to hope and order will never fully heal. Ask Argentinians or Chileans or Venezuelans or Russians or Italians—or Germans. The national psyche never gets over learning that its institutions are that fragile and their ability to resist a dictator that weak."[6] I would add, ask the Greeks who, for the last few years, have watched their precarious polity brought to the brink of disaster by their own Prime Minister Huckster Tsipras.

The larger forces of hyperpartisanship and the extraordinary profits that fuel so much of the extremism pushed on us by cable and so-called news sites suggest it will be an uphill battle. Writing in 2010, David Frum connected the dots between over-the-top rhetoric, partisan anger, and the bottom lines of media stars and companies. "When Rush Limbaugh said that he wanted President Obama to fail, he was intelligently explaining his own interests. What he omitted to say—but what is equally true—is that he also wants Republicans to fail. If Republicans succeed—if they govern successfully in office and negotiate attractive compromises out of office—Rush's listeners get less angry. And if they are less angry, they listen to the radio less, and hear fewer ads for Sleepnumber beds."[7] Could it really be that much of the Obama backlash was fuelled by one man's ever deepening, and increasingly expensive, addiction to hillbilly heroin?

As fake news becomes more sophisticated, the frothing-at-the-mouth right-wing Dittoheads of Limbaugh's era are morphing into the take-no-prisoners left-wing Retweetheads of ours. The social media mob mentality only further amplifies a rising extremism on all sides. Demagogues often leave a trashed polity behind them, and it's not the middle-of-the-road centrists who take up that space, but other populists, having learned how to manipulate a jaded, polarized public. And while cheerleaders like Milo Yiannopoulos and Richard Spencer may fall to the wayside, others, ever more finely tuned to the breathless Zeitgeist of the age of rant, like the glassy-eyed vapidities of PewDiePie or Tomi Lahren, will rise to take their place, distracting us from newly institutionalized inequities with the red-eye glare of our own outrage while the nation transforms into a land of a handful of haves blithely ignoring the mass of have-nots.

The weaponized misinformation coming out of Russia will only further degrade our communal relationship to facts warns journalist Peter Pomerantsev. "The aim is to confuse rather than convince, to trash the information space so the audience gives up looking for any truth amid the chaos."[8] And in the meantime, glued to the nonstop, 24/7 shit show that is the Trump administration, we might soon forget what measured governance is even supposed to be. "It's our growing addiction to the spectacle of his car-wreck presidency that is the real threat," warns author and journalist Matt Taibbi,[9] who himself once helped trash the common airspace in the early day's of Russia's post-Soviet democracy. "He is already making idiots and accomplices of us all, bringing out the worst in each of us, making us dumber just by watching. Even if Trump never learns to govern, after four years of this we will forget what civilization ever looked like."

The biggest threat Donald Trump poses, then, might be that he'll end our American Experiment not with a bang, but with a whimper, "steadily eroding the norms that enshrine the cautiously collaborative spirit of the American system," as *The Economist* suggests, "in which much of its defense against authoritarianism resides."[10] Steve Bannon is already looking to a future when those norms are gone, as he told Cato Institute analyst Flemming Rose last year. "Trump is just the beginning of a rebellion that will grow increasingly aggressive in the coming years," Rose wrote, describing their conversation. "In a way, [Bannon] told me, Trump is not the real thing—only a premonition of what will ultimately come. 'Just wait and see,' he said."[11]

The Road to Impeachment...?

The Justice Department special counsel—tasked with investigating the Trump campaign's collusion with Russia—Robert Mueller's Monday morning indictment of Trump's former campaign chair Paul Manafort, along with his business partner, on years-old tax and fraud charges led to a crowing Trump to declare on Twitter: "Sorry, but this is years ago, before Paul Manafort was part of the Trump campaign. But why aren't Crooked Hillary & the Dems the focus?????" But within hours, Mueller unsealed the guilty plea of former Trump foreign policy adviser and still-wet-behind-the-ears social climber[12] George Papadopoulos (causing Greek Twitter to go ablaze, as Papadopoulos was a confidant of current Minister of Defense Panos Kammenos, one of the dim bulbs over here) for lying to prosecutors about his meetings with Russians on behalf of the Trump campaign.[13]

A one-two sucker punch if ever there was one, Mueller and his team were sending a devastating message. Not only did they have the goods on former higher-ups in the Trump camp and enough to squeeze them for plea deals, they also had at least one, and maybe many more, former or current Trump stooges secretly cooperating.[14] For an already paranoia-drenched West Wing, it's like pouring oil on fire. Mueller further ramped up the pressure later that night, with his office characterizing the Papadopoulos plea as "a small part" of "a large-scale ongoing investigation."[15] Within weeks, Mueller's team announced a plea deal with the shortest-ever-serving national security adviser, Michael Flynn, on charges he lied to the FBI. While Donald Trump, and his army of echoing sycophants, claimed this as a victory, as no Russia-related charges were brought, the full impact of the plea deal remains far from clear[16], while the reported links between the Trump campaign and Russia seem to expand on an almost daily basis.[17]

Of course, Trump may yet take the scoundrel's way out, and with him bring the edifice of modern constitutional politics down around all our ears—that is, fire Mueller, as more and more Republicans are urging him to do,[18] or issue either targeted or blanket pardons for all Russia-collusion crimes, including for himself,[19] or as likely both. The *Wall Street Journal* is openly pressing the president to go down the latter path of all-out madness, citing pardons of past insurrectionists by George Washington and Abraham Lincoln, with the goal of "securing harmony in the body politic."[20] That such a harmony would be created by eviscerating that very body politic doesn't cause them so much as a quiver of anxiety. *Because hey, tax cuts for billionaires!* Trump has already performed a dry run of the scoundrel's path with his precedent-breaking pardon of ex-Sheriff Joe Arpaio in Arizona—the first case of a presidential pardon being issued before the convict was either sentenced or served a day in prison.[21]

... Or Autocracy?

David Frum predicted Donald Trump won't choose autocracy, autocracy will choose him. His need to protect his family and interests from prosecution, and his own yowling inner boy-bully's need to attack and dominate, will force him to break, brick by brick, the edifice of American democracy—saying it represents the only road for a viable presidency for a man so clearly criminally unsuited to the job.[22] And with a world tipping more giddily into global conflict, where even Japan debates whether to nuclearize,[23] the road to shredding basic freedoms and protections maybe wide open for Trump.

A war with North Korea, that escalates into a war with China, that opens Russia to larger conflicts in Europe and the Balkans, potentially destabilizing the EU and further roiling a reeling Middle East ... or any variation of the above, all adding up to, to paraphrase the man himself, *when the world goes to total hell and everything is a disaster*—will we have those riots to make us great again, or just riots, and the first, or not even first, inklings of a rising Trumpian autocratic state?

But as likely an outcome of a Trump presidency is a gradual slide into America the Kleptocrat's Paradise, where government failure and corruption, having become the norm, cause citizens to look to themselves and disparage the idea of democratically-elected bodies, or a land sunk in amnesia, where we've forgotten what it was like to live in a functioning democracy.

Imagine this: a neutered press, hated or distrusted by much of the citizenry, a State Department with endless empty halls and offices, a sidelined and demoralized national security apparatus, dismantled health, safety and consumer safeguards, bank watchdogs kowtowing solely to the interests of the monied elites and hedge fund managers, a destroyed US dollar limiting easy overseas travel to the rich, a massively ballooning deficit caused by reckless tax cuts, the end of Medicare, Medicaid, and Social Security as we know them, the loss of basic workplace and housing protections for women, minorities, and the LGBTQ community, a school system given over to for-profit corporations and church organizations, a federal judiciary packed with extreme right-wing ideologues or conspiracy-peddling hacks, a prevalent skepticism on all sides of expertise and science, hollowed-out small towns and cities as the "retail apocalypse" takes hold with a government unable or unwilling to mitigate its worst impacts, skyrocketing personal bankruptcies as Obamacare's protections are diminished or repealed, a devastated middle class sinking ever deeper into debt, and the continual fanning the flames of racial and ethnic hatred and class resentment, while reengergized white supremacists, rebranded as defenders of Trump's legacy, scapegoat Muslims, African Americans, and anyone else they choose to call the other, loudly echoing, as it does to former spook and novelist John le Carré, the rise of European fascism in the 1930s[24].

The President We Deserve Is the One We Elect?

At its heart, Donald Trump's agenda, along with those who join him in the "deconstruct the administrative state" and "Ayn Rand's America or death" wings of the Republican establishment, that ever-shifting makeup of the GOP's Neanderthal unibrow, is designed for only one thing: to initiate a genuine crisis in American governance, in the aftermath and ruins of which their ultra ultra rich buddies, those bro-tastic billionaires and Christian uberconservatives, will be able to add one, maybe two, zeros to their official *Forbes* net worth while knowing that the government they deliberately smashed is now theirs for the taking. Where that crisis takes America will depend as much on how frayed the ties that bind us as citizens have become as it does on the power of the mega-tax-cut fattened purses that want nothing better than to own this complex web we call our democracy. It is up to those of us with our double-digit donations and phone calls to senators and hand-painted protest signs and basic beliefs in humanity, generosity, and compassion to find a way to stop this.

In 1995, the novelist Steve Erickson warned how America had wearied of democracy. "History is clear that democracy cannot long navigate a sea of national rage," he wrote. "Untempered by rationale and open-mindedness, fury eventually consumes democracy rather than nourishes it, because it overwhelms our tolerance, our willingness to be reasonably informed, our determination to hold ourselves accountable for what we decide... The nation gets meaner and more petty until rage is the only national passion left—and then it is anger not at those on top, which is the anger America was born of, but at those on the bottom."[25] He could easily have been talking about America today—predicting it, even—a country riven in two, or smashed to pieces, by the competing passions and hatreds on all sides of the political spectrum.

America's promise, however it's imagined, the shining city on the hill, the Statue of Liberty with her torch guiding the world's huddled masses to our shores, or my dream of an old, weird America, is never its reality. Perhaps more than any other nation, America and we Americans have lived a fantasy on the international stage, while blindly profiting from it, offering a dream we could never deliver, endlessly gaslighting the world by the gaping chasm between who we say we are and what our actions say we are. Could it be that Donald Trump is the one truly American president we have been waiting for all these years—a messiah not of our ideals but of our earth-shackled selves—the one we both richly deserve and for whom, by our casual disregard of a polity peeling away ever more wildly from anything resembling reality, we have not only invited in but gladly handed him the keys to the kingdom? Perhaps those of us who revile Donald Trump, myself included, simply refuse to see what America has become, and in a sense always was—that the ugliness behind the mask we've told ourselves is America is all that's left of the nation.

So How Will It All End...?

Limping along, beset by scandal, new tweets endlessly twisting in the air as he spins from crisis to crisis while heedlessly slouching toward his golf club retirement, Donald Trump may yet make a fool of us all by serving out two full terms—and in Bannon's words, be only just the beginning—and it will be the demagogues or populists who take up his anguished, child's id cry in the hollowed-out, content-free polity he'll bequeath us, driving a stake into the heart of any chance of a sanity-based politics, promising the moon, or just more of the same low-wage jobs, to citizens who've largely forgotten what that means—lost to the endless distractions of the cat video industrial complex—or even what a government does or can do for its people.

To stop this, and to stop what British comic David Mitchell, referring to Brexit voters, called "people self-medicating their undiagnosed psychological problems by causing huge, ill-conceived geopolitical shifts,"[26] it'll take more than a daily barrage of retweets appropriately hashtagged or endless claims that so-and-so "Nailed it!" in 140 (or whatever) characters. Internet memes, and the nuance-free outrage they elicit, may be the morale-boosting lifeblood of the #Resistance, but they're also part of the content-free spectacle that's given us this shit show. Nor will it be the populists who save us, but the steel-hearted steady hands, genuine statesmen and women, and cold-eyed prosecutors and judges, and fearless journalists, activists and legislators, who might somehow hold us back—or pull us back—from the brink. Here's a cheer for old-fashioned grass roots democracy: showing up, organizing, protesting, donating, building coalitions, running for office, and voting.

Or we could just take Orangehead at his word[27]:

Donald J. Trump

"You can't con people, at least not for long. You can create excitement, you can do wonderful promotion and get all kinds of press, and you can throw in a little hyperbole. But if you don't deliver the goods, people will eventually catch on."

ENDNOTES

Disclaimer

[1] Philip Bump. "Trump's idea to run the government like a business is an old one in American politics," *Washington Post*, March 27, 2017.

[2] *C'mon, you really think he didn't say it?*

[3] Helena Smith. "'Patients who should live are dying': Greece's public health meltdown," *The Guardian*, January 1, 2017.

[4] John T. Psaropoulos. "Judges decry manipulation by government, media," *The New Athenian*, October 19, 2016.

[5] Luke Hurst. "Greece sees largest decline in press freedom in world," *Newsweek*, April 29, 2015.

[6] "New survey paints grim picture of shuttered businesses," *Ekathimerini*, March 23, 2017.

[7] Rachel Roberts. "Russia hired 1,000 people to create anti-Clinton 'fake news' in key US states during election, Trump-Russia hearings leader reveals," *The Independent*, March 30, 2017.

[8] Catherine Rampell. "A fraternity was told it was 'appropriating culture.' Administrators won't say which," *Washington Post*, April 20, 2017.

I. A Flash of Military Muscle

[1] Molly Fischer. "Camille Paglia Predicted 2017," *New York Magazine*, March 7, 2017.

[2] Jessica Schulberg. "Trump Sought Military Equipment For Inauguration, Granted 20-Plane Flyover," *Huffington Post*, January 19, 2017.

[3] Karen Tumulty. "How Donald Trump came up with 'Make America Great Again'," *Washington Post*, January 18, 2017.

[4] Benjy Sarlin. "Donald Trump Promises a Presidency Like No Other," NBC News, January 21, 2017.

[5]C'mon, you want a citation for this? We all effin' watched it.

[6]Michael C. Bender. "Donald Trump Strikes Nationalistic Tone in Inaugural Speech" *Wall Street Journal*, January 20, 2017.

[7]Yashar Ali. "What George W. Bush Really Thought of Donald Trump's Inauguration," *New York Magazine*, March 29, 2017.

[8]Eric Rauchway. "President Trump's 'America First' slogan was popularized by Nazi sympathizers," *Washington Post*, January 20, 2017.

II. The WrestleMania Presidency

[1]Josh Dawsey. "Trump's obsession with WrestleMania and fake drama," *Politico*, January 16, 2017.

[2]Russ Beuttner and Charles V. Bagli. "How Donald Trump Bankrupted His Atlantic City Casinos, but Still Earned Millions," *New York Times*, June 11, 2016.

[3]Dawsey.

[4]Ibid.

[5]Travis Waldron. "The Definitive History Of That Time Donald Trump Took A Stone Cold Stunner," *Huffington Post*, February 14, 2017.

[6]Benjamin Hufbauer. "How Trump's Favorite Movie Explains Him," *Politico Magazine*, June 6, 2016.

[7]Ibid.

[8]Ibid.

[9]Anthony Audi. "Errol Morris on the Time He Filmed Donald Trump Missing the Point," *Literary Hub*, October 27, 2016.

[10]Esme Crib. "Fox's Shep Smith Hits Trump On Russia Questions: 'We Have A Right To Know'," *Talking Points Memo*, February 16, 2017.

[11]Michael Goodwin. "Sorry, media—this press conference played very differently with Trump's supporters," *New York Post*, February 16, 2017.

[12]David Cantanese. "Trump Strikes Back With the Spectacle," *U.S. News & World Report*, February 16, 2017

[13]Megan Garber. "Pop Culture Resents 'The Establishment' Too," *The Atlantic*, November 16, 2016.

III. The Rise of Honey Badger

[1]David Von Drehle. "Is Steve Bannon the Second Most Powerful Man in the World?" *Time*, February 2, 2017.

[2]Ibid.

[3]Ben Shapiro. "I Know Trump's New Campaign Chairman, Steve Bannon. Here's What You Need To Know," *The Daily Wire*, November 13, 2016.

[4]Sarah Posner. "How Donald Trump's New Campaign Chief Created an Online Haven for White Nationalists," *Mother Jones*, August 22, 2016.

[5]Ibid.

[6]Von Drehle.

[7]Ibid.

[8]Ronald Radosh. "Steve Bannon, Trump's Top Guy, Told Me He Was 'A Leninist' Who Wants To 'Destroy the State'," *The Daily Beast*, August 22, 2016.

[9]Micah Sifry. " Steve Bannon Wants To Start World War III," *The Nation*, February 8, 2017.

[10]John Saward. "Steve Bannon's Sad, Desperate Crusade," *Vice*, March 20, 2017.

[11]Reid Cherlin. "The world is on fire," *Vice News*, February 15, 2017.

[12]Ibid.

[13]Neil Howe. "Where did Steve Bannon get his worldview? From my book," *Washington Post*, February 24, 2017.

[14]J. Lester Feder. "This Is How Steve Bannon Sees The Entire World," *BuzzFeed*, November 15, 206.

[15]Richard Cohen. "Trump, like Nixon, is incapable of change," *Washington Post*, February 13, 2017.

[16]Ken Stern. "Exclusive: Stephen Bannon, Trump's New C.E.O., Hints at His Master Plan," *Vanity Fair*, August 17, 2016.

IV. The Apotheosis of Ayn Rand

[1]Rachel Weiner. "Paul Ryan and Ayn Rand," *Washington Post*, August 13, 2012.

[2]Elspeth Reeve. "Audio Surfaces of Paul Ryan's Effusive Love of Ayn Rand," *The Atlantic*, April 30, 2012.

[3]James Sanford. "Why Ayn Rand Is a Fan Favorite Among Christian Theocrats," *Alternet*, June 26, 2015.

[4]Fred Barnes. "Knowledge is Power," *The Weekly Standard*, January 17, 2011.

[5]Paul A. Rahe. "Paul Ryan: A Duty to Serve," *Ricochet*, June 1, 2011.

[6]Matthew O'Brien. "Paul Ryan's Tax Math Just Became More Magical ," *The Atlantic*, March 13, 2013.

[7]Jonathan Chait. "Paul Ryan Declares War Against Math," *New York Magazine*, September 23, 2014.

[8]O'Brien.

[9]Ian Tuttle. "The Great Ignored Agenda," *National Review*, August 24, 2016.

[10]Jonathan Weisman. "Ryan's Rise From Follower to G.O.P. Trailblazer," *New York Times*, April 29, 2012.

[11]Danny Vinik. "The Ryan Budget Doesn't Just Sin Against the Poor. It Sins Against Math, Too," *New Republic*, April 11, 2014.

[12]Weisman.

[13]Ben Weyl. "Ryan plans to steamroll Democrats with budget tool," *Politico*, October 6, 2016.

[14]Weisman.

[15]Theo Anderson. "Kissing Your Way to the Top: The Paul Ryan Story," *In These Times*, July 19, 2012.

[16]David Lawler. "Donald Trump calls Paul Ryan 'weak and ineffective' and warns 'shackles taken off' him," *The Telegraph*, October 11, 2016.

[17]Mike DeBonis and Amy Phillip. "Ryan calls off plans to campaign with Trump; GOP-ers rush to distance themselves," *Washington Post*, October, 7, 2016.

[18]"Conservative Advocate," NPR *Morning Edition*, May 25, 2001.

[19]John Cassidy. "The Ringleader," *The New Yorker*, August 1, 2005.

V. Transnational Kleptocrats Unite!

[1] Richard Wolffe. "Trump's trainwreck press conference ushers in a shambolic presidency," *The Guardian*, January 12, 2107.

[2] Dan Alexander. "Ethics Experts: Trump Still Faces Serious Conflicts Of Interest," *Forbes*, January 11, 2017.

[3] Mary Papenfuss. "Donald Trump Expanding Scottish Golf Resort After Vowing Not To Make New Foreign Deals," *Huffington Post*, January 16, 2017.

[4] Amy Brittain and Drew Harwell. "Eric Trump's business trip to Uruguay cost taxpayers $97,830 in hotel bills," *Washington Post*, February 3, 2017.

[5] Eric Chemi and Nick Wells. "'Trump Cabinet index' is outpacing the market since election," CNBC, December 19, 2016.

[6] Richard Cohen. "Trump's GOP enablers take a page from the fascist-era Vatican," *Washington Post*, February 27, 2017.

[7] Dan Alexander. "Eric Trump Offers Surprisingly Candid Thoughts On Nepotism," *Forbes*, April 4, 2017.

[8] Kevin Liptak. "Trump's Secretary of Everything: Jared Kushner," CNN, April 4, 2017.

[9] Lizzie Widdicombe. "Ivanka and Jared's Power Play," *The New Yorker*, August 22, 2016.

[10] Andrew Rice. "The Young Trump," *New York Magazine*, January 8, 2017.

[11] Jason Linkins. "White House Announces Jared Kushner Is Now Responsible For Everything," *Huffington Post*, March 27, 2017.

[12] Elizabeth Spiers. "I worked for Jared Kushner. He's the wrong businessman to reinvent government," *Washington Post*, March 30, 2107.

[13] Ellen Nakashima, Adam Entous and Greg Miller. "Russian ambassador told Moscow that Kushner wanted secret communications channel with Kremlin," Washington Post, May 26, 2017.

[14] "Interview: Donald Trump," CNN *Larry King Live*, October 9, 2006.

VI. Autocracy Now

[1] David Frum. "How to Build an Autocracy," *The Atlantic*, March, 2017.

[2] Michael M. Grynbaum. "Trump Calls the News Media the 'Enemy of the American People'," *New York Times*, February 17, 2017.

[3] Frum.

[4] Chris Cillizza. "Steve Bannon's not-so-subtle threat to the media," *Washington Post*, February 23, 2017.

[5] Paul Farhi. "Journalist says Omarosa Manigault bullied her and mentioned a 'dossier' on her," *Washington Post*, February 13.

[6] Matt Shuham. "Trump Calls On Only Conservative Outlets For Three Straight Press Conferences," *Talking Points Memo*, February 15, 2017.

[7] Andrew Marantz. "Is Trump Trolling the White House Press Corps?" The New Yorker, March 20, 2017.

[8] Ari Fleischer. "Trump vs. the White House Press Corps," *Wall Street Journal*, November 28, 2016.

[9] Hadas Gold. "Russia's state news service applies for White House pass," *Politico*, March 24, 2017.

[10] Michael Scherer. "White House Bars Certain News Outlets from Daily Briefing After Trump Attack," *Time*, February 24, 2107.

[11] Frum.

[12] Ibid.

[13] Dahlia Lithwick. "Why Trump Has Declared War on the Judiciary," *Slate*, February 10, 2017.

[14] Evan Perez, Shimon Prokupecz and Ariane de Vogue. "Threats against judges in immigration ban cases leads to increased security," CNN, February 10, 2017.

[15] Lithwick.

[16] Scott Detrow. "Show's Over? Trump Pledges To Be 'So Presidential You Will Be So Bored'," NPR, April 21, 2017.

[17] Brent Kendall. "Trump Says Judge's Mexican Heritage Presents 'Absolute Conflict'," *Wall Street Journal*, June 3, 2016.

[18] George Shepherd. "The judge who saved Trump's campaign," CNN, November 18, 2016.

[19]Doina Chiacu and Julia Harte. "White House official attacks court after legal setbacks on immigration," *Reuters*, February 12, 2107.

[20]Jack Goldsmith. "Does Trump Want to Lose the EO Battle in Court? Or is Donald McGahn Simply Ineffectual (or Worse)?" *Lawfare*, February 6, 2017.

[21]Charlie Savage and Maggie Haberman. "Trump Abruptly Orders 46 Obama-Era Prosecutors to Resign," *New York Times*, March 10, 2017.

[22]Mark Hosenball. "Trump tried to call New York prosecutor before firing him—source," *Reuters*, Mach 13, 2017.

[23]Tom Hamburger. "Watchdogs ask U.S. attorney to investigate Trump over foreign business deals," *Washington Post*, March 8, 2017.

[24]Jeffrey Toobin. "The Showman," *The New Yorker*, May 9, 2016.

[25]Sari Horwitz. "A month after dismissing federal prosecutors, Justice Department does not have any U.S. attorneys in place," *Washington Post*, April 18, 2017.

VII. Voodoo to Voldemort

[1]Chris Edelson. "Ordinary Americans carried out inhumane acts for Trump," *Baltimore Sun*, February 6, 2017.

[2]"Mr. Trump's 'Deportation Force' Prepares an Assault on American Values," *New York Times*, February 21, 2017.

[3]Daniel José Camacho. "Trump's weekly list of 'immigrant crimes' is as sinister as it sounds," *The Guardian*, March 22, 2017.

[4]Sarah Kenzidor. "It's Already Happened Here," *The Baffler*, February 9, 2017.

[5]David Frum. "How to Build an Autucracy," *The Atlantic*, March, 2017.

[6]Dale Beran. "4chan: The Skeleton Key To The Rise Of Trump," *Huffington Post*, February 20, 2107.

[7]Sean McElwee. "Trump's supporters believe a false narrative of white victimhood—and the data proves it," *Salon*, February 12, 2017.

[8]John Paul Brammer. "America: behold, your Snowflake-in-Chief," *The Guardian*, January 16, 2017.

[9]Nick Bilton. "Fake News Is About to Get Even Scarier than You Ever Dreamed," *Vanity Fair*, January 26, 2017.

[10]Marc Bojanowski. "Writer Walter Kirn on Fake News, Sex Scenes and Future Robot Domination," *Playboy*, February 14, 2017.

[11]"False Stories About ICE Sweeps & Checkpoints Spark Fear In New York's Immigrant Communities," CBS New York, February 23, 2017.

[12]Ben Schreckinger. "The Alt-Right Comes to Washington," *Politico Magazine*, Jan/Feb 2017.

[13]Tristram Bridges. "Why People Are So Averse to Facts," *Sociological Images*, February 27, 2017.

[14]Julie Beck. "This Article Won't Change Your Mind," *The Atlantic*, March 13, 2107.

[15]Bilton.

VIII. Putin Picks His "Idiot"

[1]Kurt Eichenwald. "Trump, Putin and the Hidden History of How Russia Interfered in the U.S. Presidential Election," *Newsweek*, January 10, 2017.

[2]Garry Kasparov. "Trump's strange relationship: What last week revealed about the President, Putin and Russia," *New York Daily News*, February 19, 2017.

[3]*Jim Sciutto and Evan Perez*. "US investigators corroborate some aspects of the Russia dossier," CNN, February 10, 2017.

[4]Ben Guarino. "Shaking hands is 'barbaric': Donald Trump, the germaphobe in chief," *Washington Post*, January 12, 2017.

[5]Peter Stone and Greg Gordon. "FBI, 5 other agencies probe possible covert Kremlin aid to Trump," *McClatchy Report*, January 18, 2017.

[6]Glenn Kessler. "Trump's claim that 'I have nothing to do with Russia'," *Washington Post*, July 27, 2016.

[7]Tracy Wilkinson. "In a shift, Republican platform doesn't call for arming Ukraine against Russia, spurring outrage," *Los Angeles Times*, July 21, 2016.

[8]Oren Dorrell. "Russian ambassador Sergey Kislyak leaves trail of U.S. election meddling," *USA Today*, March 2, 2017.

[9]Eliza Relman and Natasha Bertrand. "Paul Manafort is now at the center of the Trump-Russia investigation—here's what you need to know about him," *Business Insider*, March 24, 2017.

[10]Franklin Foer. "The Quiet American," *Slate*, April 28, 2016.

[11]Glenn Thrush. "To Charm Trump, Paul Manafort Sold Himself as an Affordable Outsider," *New York Times*, April 8, 2017.

[12]Josh Marshall. "This Article Doesn't Talk It Screams," *Talking Points Memo*, April 10, 2017.

[13]Kenneth P. Vogel, David Stern and Josh Meyer. "Manafort's Ukrainian 'blood money' caused qualms, hack suggests," *Politico*, February 28, 2017.

[14]Natasha Bertrand. "Hacked text messages allegedly sent by Paul Manafort's daughter discuss 'blood money' and killings, and a Ukrainian lawyer wants him to explain," *Business Insider*, March 21, 2107.

[15]Dana Bash, Theodore Schleifer and Ashley Killough. "Donald Trump campaign chairman Paul Manafort resigns," CNN, August 20, 2016.

[16]Ashley Feinberg. "Hacked Texts Suggest Manafort Continued to Play a Role After Departing Trump Campaign," *The Slot*, March 21, 2017.

[17]"Associated Press Investigation Says Paul Manafort Worked With Russian Billionaire," NPR *Morning Edition*, March 22, 2017.

[18]Jeff Horwitz and Chad Day. "AP Exclusive: Before Trump job, Manafort worked to aid Putin," Associated Press, March 22, 2017.

[19]Jordyn Phelps and Adam Kelsey. "Spicer: Former campaign chairman had 'very limited role'," ABC News, March 20, 2017.

[20]Matthew Rosenberg and Maggie Haberman."Michael Flynn, Anti-Islamist Ex-General, Offered Security Post, Trump Aide Says," *New York Times*, November 16, 2016.

[21]James Kitfield. "How Mike Flynn Became America's Angriest General," *Politico*, October 16, 2016.

[22]Ibid.

[23]Natasha Bertrand. "The timeline of Trump's ties with Russia lines up with allegations of conspiracy and misconduct," *Business Insider*, February 11, 2017.

[24]Matthew Rosenberg and Maggie Haberman, "Michael Flynn, Anti-Islamist Ex-General, Offered Security Post, Trump Aide Says," *New York Times*, November 17, 2016.

25"Trump suggests he may do away with Russia sanctions if Moscow helpful: WSJ," *Reuters*, January 14, 2017.

26Tim Lister. "Who is Sergey Kislyak, the Russian ambassador to the United States?" CNN, March 2, 2017

27"Gen. Michael Flynn Spoke To Russian Ambassador Same Day Sanctions Were Announced," NPR *Weekend Edition*, January 14, 2017.

28Jonathan Landay and Arshad Mohammed. "Trump adviser had five calls with Russian envoy on day of sanctions: sources," *Reuters*, January 23, 2017.

29Emily Schultheis. "Mike Pence says Trump adviser's contact with Russia was 'strictly coincidental'," CBS *Face the Nation*, January 15, 2017.

30Kurt Eichenwald. "Why the Flynn-Russia Affair Is So Troubling for Donald Trump," *Newsweek*, February 21, 2107

31Michael Hayden. "Former CIA chief: Trump is Russia's useful fool," *Washington Post*, November 3, 2016.

32Michael V. Hayden. "Former CIA chief: Trump is Russia's useful fool," *Washington Post*, November 3, 2016.

33Sophie Tatum. "Trump defends Putin: 'You think our country's so innocent?'," CNN, February 6, 2017. (http://edition.cnn.com/2017/02/04/politics/donald-trump-vladimir-putin/)

34Del Quentin Wilber. "Follow the money and the trail of 'dead Russians,' expert urges senators ," *Los Angeles Times*, March 30, 2017

35Bill Palmer. "Meet the nine Russian operatives who have dropped dead during Donald Trump-Russia scandal," *Palmer Report*, March 12, 2017

36Hayden.

IX. Count Your Holy Wars

1Hunter Walker. "Donald Trump has big plans for 'radical Islamic' terrorists, 2016 and 'that communist' Bernie Sanders," *Yahoo News*, November 19, 2015.

2David Muir. "Transcript: ABC News anchor David Muir interviews President Trump," ABC News, January 25, 2017.

[3]Jeremy Diamond. "Trump: Defense Secretary Mattis can 'override' me on torture," CNN, January 27, 2017.

[4]Jeremy Diamond. "Trump cites story of general who dipped bullets in pigs' blood to deter Muslims," CNN, February 20, 2016.

[5]Michael Gerson. "Bannon's reckless pursuit of ethno-nationalist greatness," *Washington Post*, February 27, 2017.

[6]J. Lester Feder. "This Is How Steve Bannon Sees The Entire World," *BuzzFeed*, November 15, 2016.

[7]Quoted in Gerson.

[8]Jennifer Rubin. "Bannon and Trump are out for revenge," *Washington Post*, February 24, 2017.

[9]Garry Kasparov. "Trump's strange relationship: What last week revealed about the President, Putin and Russia," *New York Daily News*, February 19, 2017.

[10]"Trump: We have to start winning wars again," CNN *Newsroom*, February 27, 2017.

[11]W.J. Hennigan. "Trump administration stops disclosing troop deployments in Iraq and Syria," *Los Angeles Times*, March 30, 2017.

[12]Dan De Luce, Paul McLeary. "Trump's Ramped-Up Bombing in Yemen Signals More Aggressive Use of Military," *Foreign Policy*, March 9, 2017.

[13]Pamela Engel. "Donald Trump: 'I would bomb the s--- out of' ISIS," *Business Insider*, November 13, 2015.

[14]Jason Le Miere. "Under Trump, U.S. Military Has Allegedly Killed Over 1,000 Civilians in Iraq, Syria in March," *Newsweek*, March 31, 2017.

[15]Scott Shane, Matthew Rosenberg and Eric Lipton. "Trump Pushes Dark View of Islam to Center of U.S. Policy-Making," *New York Times*, February 1, 2017.

[16]Scott Shane. "Stephen Bannon in 2014: We Are at War With Radical Islam," *New York Times*, February 1, 2017.

[17]Peter Walker. "Steve Bannon thinks an apocalyptic third world war is coming, claims historian," *The Independent*, February 9, 2107.

[18]Benjamin Hass. "Steve Bannon: 'We're going to war in the South China Sea ... no doubt'," *The Guardian*, February 2, 2017.

[19]Tracy Wilkinson. "Trump's plans to scuttle or amend the Iran nuclear deal remain a work in progress," *Los Angeles Times*, November 14, 2016.

[20]Hass.

[21]David Brunnstrom and Matt Spetalnick. "Tillerson says China should be barred from South China Sea islands," *Reuters*, January 12, 2107.

[22]Liu Zhen. "China 'steps up preparedness for possible military conflict with US'," *South China Morning Post*, January 27, 2017.

[23]Graham Allison. "How Trump and China's Xi could stumble into war," *Washington Post*, March 31, 2017.

[24]Jon Sharman. "US would go into any war with China with 'unparalleled violence', warn experts," *The Independent*, February 5, 2017.

[25]Kasparov.

[26]Sarah Kenzidor. "Trump and Putin: The worst case scenario," *Quartz*, December 23, 2016.

[27]Lois Romano. "Donald Trump, Holding All The Cards—The Tower! The Team! The Money! The Future!" *Washington Post*, November 15, 1984.

[28]Glenn Plaskin. "Playboy Interview: Donald Trump," *Playboy*, March, 1990.

[29]Matthew J. Belvedere. "Trump asks why US can't use nukes: MSNBC," CNBC, August 3, 2016.

[30]Chris Matthews. "Donald Trump won't take nuclear weapons off the table," MSNBC *Hardball with Chris Matthews*, March 30, 2016.

X. Revenge of the Basement Trolls

[1]Jack Hunter. "Meet Milo Yiannopoulos, the Appealing Young Face of the Racist Alt-Right," *The Daily Beast*, May 5, 2016.

[2]Dale Beran. "4chan: The Skeleton Key To The Rise Of Trump," *Huffington Post*, February 20, 2107.

[3]Ibid.

[4]Ben Schreckinger. "The Alt-Right Comes to Washington," *Politico Magazine*, Jan/Feb 2017.

[5]Daniel Lombroso and Yoni Appelbaum. "'Hail Trump!': White Nationalists Salute the President-Elect," *The Atlantic*, November 21, 2016.

[6] Schreckinger.

[7]Jason Horowitz. "Steve Bannon Cited Italian Thinker Who Inspired Fascists," *New York Times*, February 10, 2017.

[8]Lombroso and Appelbaum.
[9]Horowitz.
[10]Ibid.
[11]Ibid.

XI. Wagner on the Turntable

[1]SemDem. "Yes, Trump's Aide Really Did Throw 'White Power' Sign," *DailyKos*, February 22, 2017.
[2]Fernando Peinado. "How White House advisor Stephen Miller went from pestering Hispanic students to designing Trump's immigration policy," Univision, February 8, 2017.
[3]Ibid.
[4]Ibid.
[5]Lisa Mascaro. "How a liberal Santa Monica high school produced a top Trump advisor and speechwriter," *Los Angeles Times*, January 17, 2017.
[6]Glenn Thrush and Jennifer Steinhauer. "Stephen Miller Is a 'True Believer' Behind Core Trump Policies," *New York Times*, February 11, 2017
[7]"Top Trump aide wears medal of Hungarian Nazi collaborators," *Times of Israel*, February 14, 2017.
[8]Allegra Kirkland. "Did Gorka Really Wear A Medal Linked To Nazi Ally To Trump Inaugural Ball?" *Talking Points Memo*, February 13, 2017.
[9]Ibid.
[10]Chris Massie. "WH official: We'll say 'fake news' until media realizes attitude of attacking the President is wrong," CNN, February 7, 2017.
[11]Publius Decius Mus. "The Flight 93 Election," *Claremont Review of Books*, Septermber 5, 2016.
[12]Ibid.
[13]Publius Decius Mus. "Toward a Sensible, Coherent Trumpism," *Unz Review*, March 10, 2016.
[14]Ibid.

XII. Donald Does Berlin

[1]"Interview: Donald Trump," CNN *Larry King Live*, October 15, 2007.)

[2]Fareed Zakaria. "The Rise of Illiberal Democracy," *Foreign Affairs*, Nov/Dec, 1997.

[3]Gideon Rachman. "The authoritarian wave reaches the west," *Financial Times*, February 20, 2017.

[4]Ibid.

[5]Anne Applebaum. "Illiberal democracy comes to Poland," *Washington Post*, December 22, 2016.

[6]Zoltan Simon. "Orban Says He Seeks to End Liberal Democracy in Hungary," *Bloomberg*, July 28, 2014.

[7]Associated Press. "Watchdog report: 'Breakdown of democracy' in Poland, Hungary," *The Malta Independent*, April 4, 2017.

[8]Tezcan Gumus. "Turkey is about to use democracy to end its democracy," *Quartz*, April 5, 2017.

[9]Rainer Buergin and Toluse Olorunnipa. "Trump Slams NATO, Floats Russia Nuke Deal in European Interview," *Bloomberg*, January 16, 2017.

[10]Harriet Agerholm. "Brexit: Donald Trump 'could tempt other countries to leave EU if he strikes favourable US-UK deal'," *The Independent*, January 16, 2017.

[11]Kamal Ahmed. "Euro 'could fail', says man tipped as US ambassador to EU," BBC News, January 25, 2017.

[12]"Merkel, responding to Trump, says Europe's fate is in its own hands," *Reuters*, January 17, 2017.

[13]Ian Wishart and Patrick Donahue. "EU to Trump: Mess With Brexit and We'll Mess With Texas," *Bloomberg*, Masrch 30, 2017.

[14]Harold James. "Trump's Currency War Against Germany Could Destroy the EU," *Foreign Policy*, February 2, 2017.

[15]Fareed Zakaria. "America's democracy has become illiberal," *Washington Post*, December 29, 2016.

[16]Tim Skoczek. "McCain: No comparison between Trump and Reagan," CNN, April 2, 2017.

XIII. Billionaires Gotta Billionaire

[1] Matthew Rozsa. "#DrainTheSwamp: Donald Trump's Cabinet of billionaires is worth more than a third of all Americans," *Salon*, December 16, 2016.

[2] Matea Gold, Drew Harwell and Jenna Johnson. "Trump's closest aides hail from ranks of financial elite," Washington Post, April 1, 2017.

[3] Niamh McIntyre. "Activists tricked Trump supporters into waving Russian flags at CPAC," *The Independent*, February 25, 2017.

[4] Richard Wolffe. "Steve Bannon lifted his mask of death at CPAC. It wasn't a pretty sight," *The Guardian*, February 23, 2017.

[5] Z. Byron Wolf. "Steve Bannon outlines his plan to 'deconstruct' Washington," CNN, February 24, 2017.

[6] Max Fisher. "Stephen K. Bannon's CPAC Comments, Annotated and Explained," *New York Times*, February 24, 2017.

[7] Philip Bump. "Trump's idea to run the government like a business is an old one in American politics," *Washington Post*, March 27, 2017.

[8] Gregory Krieg. "What the 'deconstruction of the administrative state' really looks like," CNN, March 30, 2017.

[9] Louis Nelson. "Mulvaney: Proposed cuts to Meals on Wheels are compassionate to taxpayers," *Politico*, March 16, 2017.

XIV. Goodbye, America?

[1] "Interview: Donald Trump," Fox News *Fox & Friends*, February, 2014.

[2] Alan Rappeport. "Consumer Watchdog Faces Attack by House Republicans," *New York Times*, February 9, 2017.

[3] "Interview: Elaine Chao," Fox News *Hannity*, February 28, 2017.

[4] Carl Pope. "The Most Dangerous Bill You've Never Heard Of Just Passed The House," *Huffington Post*, January 10 2017.

[5] Victoria Herrmann. "I am an Arctic researcher. Donald Trump is deleting my citations," *The Guardian*, March 28, 2017.

[6] Emily Atkin. "The White House says it's 'not familiar' with the economic impacts of climate change," *New Republic*, March 29, 2017

[7]Juliet Eilperin, Chris Mooney and Steven Mufson. "New EPA documents reveal even deeper proposed cuts to staff and programs," *Washington Post*, March 31, 2017.

[8]Charlie May. "Paul Ryan aims for Medicare, Medicaid, Social Security cuts in 2018," *Salon*, December 7, 2017.

[9]Chris Mooney. "Trump aims deep cuts at energy agency that helped make solar power affordable," *Washington Post*, March 31, 2017.

[10]"'I love the poorly educated' — Read Donald Trump's full Nevada victory speech," *Quartz*, February 24, 2016.

[11]Helin Jung. "11 Things You Need to Know About Betsy DeVos, Secretary of Education," *Cosmopolitan*, February 7, 2017.

[12]Kristina Rizga. "Betsy DeVos Wants to Use America's Schools to Build 'God's Kingdom'," *Mother Jones*, Mar/Apr 2017.

[13]Dan Alexander. "Betsy DeVos Says It's 'Possible' Her Family Has Donated $200M To Republicans," *Forbes*, January 17, 2017.

[14]Jane Mayer. "Betsy DeVos, Trump's Big-Donor Education Secretary," *The New Yorker*, November 23, 2016.

Afterword

[1]So say the Internets, and who doesn't believe the Internets?

[2]Abbe Gluck. "President Trump Admits He's Trying to Kill Obamacare," *Vox*, October 17, 2017.

[3]Josh Hoxie. "Trump's Tax Cuts are the Biggest Wealth Grab in Modern History," *Fortune*, November 3, 2017.

[4] Tina Nguyen. "John Kelly, in Spicer Moment, Calls Robert E. Lee an 'Honorable Man'." *Vanity Fair*, October 30, 2017.

[5]David Nakamura and Aaron C. Davis. "After Charlottesville, Trump retweets — then deletes — image of train running over CNN reporter, *Washington Post*, August 15, 2017.

[6]Adam Gopnik. "The Dangerous Acceptance of Donald Trump." *The New Yorker*, May 20, 2016.

[7]David Frum. "Waterloo," *Frum Forum*, March 21, 2010.

[8]Peter Pomerantsev. "Inside Putin's Information War," *Politico Magazine*, January 4, 2015.

[9]Matt Taibbi. "Trump the Destroyer," *Rolling Stone,* March 22, 2017.

[10] "America's system of checks and balances might struggle to contain a despot," *The Economist*, February 4, 2017.

[11]Flemming Rose. "I Told Steve Bannon: 'We Are Not At War With Islam.' He Disagreed," *Huffington Post,* February 14, 2017.

[12]Alexis Papachelas. "The ambitious George Papadopoulos," *Ekathimerini,* November 7, 2017.

[13]Chris Cilizza. "Why George Papadopoulos' guilty plea is a much bigger problem for Trump than the Manafort indictment," CNN, October 30, 2017.

[14]Ibid.

[15]Katelyn Polantz. "Special counsel's office: Papadopoulos 'small part' of 'large scale investigation'," CNN October 30, 2017.

[16]Susan Hennessey and Benjamin Wittes. "The Unsolved Mystery of Michael Flynn's plea Deal," *Foreign Policy*, December 8, 2107.

[17]Rosalind S. Helderman, Tom Hamburger and Carol D. Leonnig. "At least nine people in Trump's orbit had contact with Russians during campaign and transition," Washington Post, November 5, 2017.

[18]Joe Perticone. "Republicans just introduced a resolution to remove Mueller from the Trump-Russia investigation," Business Insider, November 3, 2017.

[19]Jakob Frenkel. "President Trump Can Preemptively Pardon His Advisers And Family, But Will He?" *Forbes,* July 21, 2017.

[20]David B. Rivkin Jr. and Lee A. Casey. "Begging Your Pardon, Mr. President," Wall Street Journal, October 29, 2017.

[21]Kevin Liptak, Daniella Diaz and Sophie Tatum. "Trump pardons former Sheriff Joe Arpaio," CNN, August 27, 2017.

[22]David Frum. "How to Build an Autucracy," *The Atlantic*, March, 2017.

[23]Tom O'Connor. "North Korea Threat Pushes Japan to Talk Nuclear Weapons, but History Stops Trump Ally From Building a Bomb," *Newsweek,* November 6, 2017.

[24]Mark Brown. "John le Carré on Trump: 'Something seriously bad is happening'," *The Guardian*, September 7, 2017.

[25]Steve Erickson. "American Weimar," *Los Angeles Times Sunday Magazine,* January 8, 1995.

[26]David Mitchell. "Unhappy Ukippers? Maybe Europe wasn't the issue…," *The Guardian*, April 2, 2017.

[27]Or damn, this mofo is going down or we are fucked.

About the Author

As a twelve year-old in London, Ranbir Sidhu was one of the youngest organizers for the Campaign for Nuclear Disarmament, and later, as a newly-minted American teenager, he campaigned for Walter Mondale and Geraldine Ferraro in the 1984 election and also volunteered for the Green Party and anti-nuclear and anti-apartheid movements. His interest in American politics has remained steady since. He is the author of three previous books, *Deep Singh Blue*, a novel, *Object Lessons*, a novella, and *Good Indian Girls*, a collection of stories, and he is a winner of the Pushcart Prize in fiction and a New York Foundation for the Arts Fellowship, among other awards. He currently lives in Greece. Connect with him at ranbirsidhu.com.

Printed in the USA
CPSIA information can be obtained
at www.ICGtesting.com
JSHW022337140824
68134JS00019B/1537

9 781944 700782